STABLE

STABLE

THE KEYS TO
HEAVEN ON EARTH

APRIL MICHELLE LEWIS

InspiringVoices®

ISBN: 978-1-4624-0471-1 (sc)
ISBN: 978-1-4624-0472-8 (e)

Library of Congress Control Number: 2012923340

Inspiring Voices books may be ordered through booksellers or by contacting:

Inspiring Voices
1663 Liberty Drive
Bloomington, IN 47403
www.inspiringvoices.com
1-(866) 697-5313

Because of the dynamic nature of the Internet, any web addresses or links contained in this book may have changed since publication and may no longer be valid. The views expressed in this work are solely those of the author and do not necessarily reflect the views of the publisher, and the publisher hereby disclaims any responsibility for them.

Any people depicted in stock imagery provided by Thinkstock are models, and such images are being used for illustrative purposes only.

Certain stock imagery © Thinkstock.

Print information available on the last page.

Inspiring Voices rev. date: 04/27/2017

To God, my heavenly Father, for the love you have shown me and the peace and joy you have given to me. My love for you is endless.
To my husband, who has shown me his unconditional love.
To all of my children, who have taught me that love has no boundaries.
To Mom and Dad, for their lessons of faith.
And to all of you, for believing in me.

True love never dies.

This is life that lasts forever. It is to know You, the only true God. — John 17:3 (New Life Version)

Contents

Chapter One

What Is STABLE?

stable—('stei bel) not likely to fall or give way; firmly established; enduring; permanent; not wavering in character; having the ability to react to a disturbing force by maintaining an established position.
— Random House Webster's College Dictionary

If you are reading this book, surely it is because you are searching for answers to many of life's questions. Perhaps you are searching for God, truth, or a definite description of your own spirituality. Maybe you just want to understand the true existence of heaven in its own tangible form. Perhaps you just picked up this book because you are simply going through a rough time or situation in your life. Whether you are searching for peace or, at the very least, are just curious to hear what I have to say, I thank you so much for taking the time to read this book.

I would like to take this opportunity to introduce myself, summarize what has happened in my life, and explain how the STABLE philosophy came to be.

I am a forty-year-old housewife, writer, and speaker. I have five beautiful children—three of my own and two stepchildren. Right out of the gate, I confess that I am not a minister or pastor, nor do I lead any type of religious movement. I believe in one truth and feel compelled to share this with you. We are all looking for truth in its purest form. My wish is that by the end of this book, you will understand what STABLE means and how it all came together. I aspire for it to bless you in some way and to help you in your own life. Ultimately, it is my goal to provide you with the absolute truth.

I have been through a lot of devastating "stuff," as most of us have. I have seen loved ones suffer from alcoholism, drug abuse, and severe depression, which had a profound impact on me during my formative years. In my thirties, I had a life-changing experience that sent me to the deepest levels of rock bottom. I lost everything I had ever worked for, and I needed to rebuild my life from nothing. At that time, I experienced unrelenting and debilitating depression that nearly caused me to take my own life.

I was so desperate to heal myself of this sadness and to find happiness once again. My heart and mind felt irreversibly damaged, and I thought I would never be the same. I wanted to heal my mind and heart and was hurting both mentally and physically. For years, I felt utterly paralyzed and could not even think clearly. And so I began an amazing journey to put my shattered life back together, bit by tiny bit.

As I painstakingly tried to clean up the mess of my life, I began to analyze the concepts of happiness, peace, and joy. I observed that in this world, there are themes of joy and happiness everywhere we go, especially during the holidays, when we receive greeting cards with phrases like "joy to the world" or "peace on earth." I eagerly wanted to know how one goes about finding that happiness and joy we all wish for each other, and I needed to know how to obtain them. Despite the many resources available to help me, I felt as if I needed a more practical approach than just counseling or medication.

Happiness was not some silly cliché to me; I took the goal of finding it very seriously. So in my grief, the wheels in my mind started turning, and I found myself consumed with questions like "How *do* I get happy?" and "Is there some formula besides taking an antidepressant to get there?" From my perspective, it seemed that everyone in the whole world was singing happy holiday songs and wishing one another peace and joy when all I ever perceived from all around me was depression, frustration, and conflict. And so I began to ponder, "Is joy something we just blurt out and pretend to possess? Secretly, are we just a bunch of phonies and none of us can actually obtain joy?" I needed to know. I had an insatiable hunger to find out how to be happy once and for all. This is what I want to share with you.

I grasped at anything I could to become the happy and healthy person I had once been. I listened to spiritual teachers and motivational speakers. I read self-help books. I went to psychiatrists and psychologists. I studied yoga. You name it, I did it. I even ended up going to graduate school to study psychology. This process of personal study went on for many years. I studied and studied and studied each expert's particular angle on how to find inner peace and happiness. From this process, what happened to me was so profound—something I never would have anticipated. Not only did healing begin to take place in my mind and heart but also a significant creation of my own philosophy took shape.

I gradually discovered universal connections between what scientists, religious teachers, philosophers, yogis, motivational speakers, and even musicians were saying. It started clicking with me over the years that everyone who offers a message of peace and happiness is virtually saying the same thing but in his or her own words and with a certain spin. A spiritual teacher may say it differently from a psychologist, and a psychologist may say it differently from a yogi master, and a yogi master may say it a little bit differently from the self-help book, but there is a universal connection among all of the messages. And there is nothing wrong with that. For me, it was a significant and profound observation that you will understand once you finish reading this book.

Let me explain how STABLE began to develop. I am a Christian. I believe in Jesus Christ as my Savior, and I believe in His messages. Every time I heard or read about His character—even how He came into this world—I heard the word *stable*, which just jumped off the pages to me. I decided I would use this word to explain how people can heal and fully live.

Organized religion and churches can certainly perform wonderful works in this world. I, however, got so discouraged by going to church every Sunday, coming home, and still feeling miserable, and I repeated this cycle weekly. I recited the same hymns and creeds over and over every week and still had problems with relationships, negativity, materialism, and frustration. I followed religious laws and traditions, but I was still filled with anger and resentment. That is not the point of Jesus Christ's message. I know that now because now I have really learned. Unfortunately, however, many of us live our lives as I once did.

I continued analyzing all aspects of my life while listening to many different types of teachers. I started noticing that my daughter's T-shirts had messages of love, hope, and peace on them because they were popular in young girls' fashion. How was it that I could turn on any popular music station and find that the common themes of the songs were love, relationships, and even believing in one's self? How was it that I could read an article in a medical journal about how forgiveness is actually healthy for our physical bodies? I was asking these questions because I did not understand how pop culture, the sciences, various religions, and so on all teach such wonderful, common messages, and yet we still remain in an "us versus them" world. Why are we so segregated?

Virtually all religions, spiritual teachers, motivational speakers, psychologists, and themes in our popular culture promote common goals of love, forgiveness, altruism, and healthy relationships. Yet within each core religion, there are different sets of rules, various traditions, and slightly different versions of the same basic teachings that create an "I am right, you are wrong" mentality, which, in turn, feeds the very *opposite* of the basic teachings by promoting hate, prejudice, and even killing. As a result, unfortunately, many have developed a distaste for and frustration with organized religions of the world. For these reasons, God Himself is wrongly and undeservedly criticized and thrown out of mainstream society and institutions.

Messages of hope and love are everywhere in our world. So I raise the question: Why has the world become so incredibly divided when everyone seems to possess all the passion and drive to speak, sing, and teach about the same thing? Why the disconnect? Are not the hate, judgment, and segregation the very antithesis of the commonly portrayed message?

I believe that Jesus Christ is one of the most misunderstood messengers in all of history and that His teachings have become convoluted, miscommunicated, and carried out in ways that conflict with His original teachings. He passionately felt that organized religion was futile if we do not love one another, forgive, and help our fellow man. When He lived here on earth, He associated himself with *everyone*. His heart was filled with unconditional love and compassion for *all* mankind, and He certainly was not one to associate only with those He considered His "own kind." Later in this book, and as we explore the STABLE philosophy further, I will elaborate more on this topic.

I came to the pinnacle of my own personal studies where I felt an incredible sense of purpose to ask humankind these crucial questions: Why are we judging each other?

Why do we hate each other? Why do we fight each other when the underlying messages everywhere we go are the same? In 1981, James Fowler, author of *Stages of Faith: The Psychology of Human Development and the Quest for Meaning,* elaborated on this most perfectly. He described how we all reach a point when we realize that religions all have the same basic core truths. It is time for the wool to be pulled from our eyes and realize that we, as *one world,* are actually on the same page. Many have expressed similar beliefs.

So there you have it. All that I have just explained to you are merely the questions that have kept me awake at night for a very long time. They were only the beginning of the thought processes that would aid in forming what is now my philosophy. As time went by, two final pieces of the puzzle really brought it all together for me.

The Pope's Question and the Lord's Prayer

In my personal search for peace and happiness, I found myself reading constantly as I grasped for any bit of advice or information that could help me. In all of my fervent reading, I came across an article about the Roman Catholic Pope. Upon reading it, I had one of those aha moments. I said to myself, "Wow, this really answers it all! I really have to address this!" I will explain.

In May of 2011, Pope Benedict XVI had a conversation with astronauts aboard the International Space Station. In this unique conversation, the Pope first commented, "I think it must be obvious to you how we all live together on *one* earth and how absurd it is that we fight and kill one another." He then asked this history-making question of the astronauts: "Do you ever wonder about the way nations and people live together down here, about how science can contribute to the cause of peace?" The astronauts answered that their work in space was a collaboration of fifteen nations. For some reason, and I have felt this way ever since I first read the article, I have been completely consumed by and compelled to address his question. I know that no one had asked me to chime in, but I just felt that I must. Slowly, I came across more and more information that contributed to my answer to this question. Later in this book, I will describe and explain how scientists, researchers, and psychologists can now validate godly principles in their truest sense and ultimately create peace, not just in our individual lives but, yes, for the entire world. So let us hold this thought for now.

The second thing that provided the very foundation for STABLE was a phrase found in the Lord 's Prayer. One day, as I was randomly speaking this prayer, one phrase suddenly jumped out at me as if I were struck by lightning. It began to play over and over in my mind as I began to analyze it. A verse in the Lord's Prayer says, "Thy will be done in earth, as it is in heaven." I want you to just think about that for a moment: if you've ever said that prayer, even if you have not, I ask that you just think about it anyway. Stop reading for a moment and, please, just meditate on this very thought. I must ask you, do we really understand what we are asking for? Millions upon millions of times this prayer has been recited over a couple of thousand years. I know that, personally, when I say a prayer, you can bet that I expect an answer! Don't you think that it is time for the Lord's Prayer to be answered? Don't you think that it is time that we start living here on earth in such a way that is in accordance with the will of heaven? I most certainly do.

"Thy will be done in earth, as it is in heaven" does not mean that one sect of one organized religion lives out its brand or adopted version of heaven here on earth. Answering this prayer means taking a look at the physical realities of the afterlife that we cannot change no matter how we label ourselves and starting to live out the characteristics of that reality while we are in these bodies. It applies to every single human being here on earth.

That phrase in the Lord's Prayer and the answer to Pope Benedict XVI's question really are the main points of this entire book, my entire message, and the very footing on which the STABLE philosophy stands. *It is time* for answers. We as *one world* have the ability to facilitate the solutions. So many of us are tired of reciting the same prayers as if we are reciting the alphabet. *It is time* to start realizing what we are asking for and taking very serious action, not as a branded religion, but as a united human race.

> *I gave them this glory so that they can be one, the same as you and I are one.*
> — Jesus's prayer to God in John 17:22 (ERV)

9

Dr. Jeffrey Long and His Scientific Research

Having stressed the significance of the Pope's question regarding how science can contribute to peace on earth and also pondering God's will in heaven and how it may be manifested here on this planet, I point now in the direction of Dr. Jeffrey Long and his scientific research. First, we must begin to understand the realities of the afterlife before we can live them out in the here and now. In 1998 Dr. Long established the Near-Death Experience Research Foundation. In addition, he recently published a best-selling book based on his research entitled *Evidence of the Afterlife*. He has encountered patient after patient who has died and been medically revived. *Death* here is defined as an absence of breath, heartbeat, and brain activity. Countless times, he has observed similarities in the stories of these near-death case studies, stories that prompted him to begin this formal research. He, however, is not alone. Many other researchers and scientists have studied millions of individuals who have reported strikingly similar near-death experiences.

As discussed in the previous section, Pope Benedict XVI posed a question that, if it can really be answered, has the ability to transform the way humankind operates in this world. The scientific study of near-death experiences is significant in this context. I emphatically state that Dr. Jeffrey Long is *the* type of scientist—or even *the* scientist—that can answer the Pope's question. I will explain. The Pope asked how science can contribute to peace on earth. Well, let us look at what Dr. Jeffrey Long is really studying. He is studying what happens to us when we pass from these physical bodies and leave this earth. His findings and those of other psychiatrists and researchers, such as Elisabeth Kubler-Ross, Bruce Greyson, and Ray Moody, to name a few, are consistent across Western and Eastern cultures, both genders, all religious sects, various races, and various ages. Research has shown that individuals who have died, who brains show absolutely no activity whatsoever, have experienced the most lucid, sensational, and realistic experiences of their entire lives with an overwhelming sense of love and joy that they themselves cannot fully express in human terms. They begin to feel great concern for their relationships and how they have treated others. They bring these experiences back for us all, similar stories retold over and over. Those who disbelieve have futilely disputed these glorious findings by making claims that, in the dying stage, the mind, even though inactive and dead to modern instruments, is overcome with a rush of endorphins or mulls over final thoughts and memories. They are not able to explain, however, how these individuals who have passed on and returned can instantly explain things that they would not otherwise be able to know, such as communications between their rescuers, activity in other locations, or information about other deceased individuals. Nor have they been able to provide any explanation as to why these afterlife experiences are described as more vivid and realistic than anything experienced in the physical realm on earth.

The study of the near-death experience is the science that we must all pay attention to as one entire, united world. *It is time* that we had enough of our various rules, wars, judging, segregation, and hate. We must take a very serious look at what happens to us when we leave this earth. We all have a birth experience, we all have a life experience, and we all have a physical death experience. This is not something that we can label or brand like Coke versus Pepsi. Just like I cannot command my digestive system to work any differently from anyone else's, death is also a real, physical, and biological process that cannot be made to play out differently from that of any other human being. Let us use this science to discover truth and really come to understand the very nature of God. People who have died and lived to tell their stories offer us incredible discovery. Let the discoveries of love, forgiveness, and how we treat others validate the original message of Jesus Christ and what he was trying to tell us. Let it also validate the core values of teachings that we hear everywhere, from all religions of the world. Let us use this science to unite us.

> *Make them ready for your service through your truth. Your [God's] teaching is truth.*
> — John 17:17 (ERV)

I know for a fact that most of the people in this world want something to be proven to them scientifically before they believe it to be truth. It does not matter what it is. We accept cures for diseases, technology and innovation, scientific discoveries of the human mind, and so on as truthful knowledge based on research. Science is based on testing and the scientific method. When the same, consistent results are manifested repeatedly, they are then written in stone—or medical and scientific journals, more specifically—and we call them knowledge or truth. The research and findings of near-death experiences are no different.

Let us now explore Dr. Long's research and exactly what he and others like him have discovered. The following are quotes from the book *Evidence of the Afterlife*, and they are just two examples out of millions. All of Dr. Long's studies focused on different genders, cultures, and ages. Each participant had his or her own unique verbal portrayal of the experience. However, they all essentially described the same experience of love, acceptance, and concern over how they treated others while they were alive. It did not matter how much money they had, what kind of cars they drove, or the sizes of their houses. None of these things seemed to matter as they passed on. They simply felt love to a degree they had never felt before.

One participant said, "Consciously living by love is the essence of life itself. I felt the total embrace of love. I was happy [and] peaceful and desired to stay. The sensation I felt I cannot express in words, but it was wonderfully tranquilizing." Another stated, "There wasn't anything that I wanted more than to stay. Pure love is the best way to describe the being and place that I would be leaving. Under protest I was sent back. I found that my purpose would be to live 'heaven on earth' using this new understanding and also to share this knowledge with other people."

Reports such as these are repeated in near-death studies over and over again.

Think about that phrase, "Consciously living by love is the essence of life itself." The Bible also says, "Above all, clothe yourselves with love which binds us all together in perfect harmony" (Col. 3:14 NLT). So you see, connections between science and God's messages of love exist. I hope now that you are beginning to understand the direction in which I am taking you. The key to everything is love—love in *all* we do; accepting and loving ourselves in a healthy and humble way; loving and thinking of others in all we do and say; loving our God, our Creator; loving Him enough to fulfill our purpose here on earth. If we so badly want to live as though heaven is on earth, then we need to examine the very nature of the closest thing we have to heaven. Why wait? Why stumble through this life on earth only to find out too late what we could have, should have, been doing when we were living? Why waste truth and knowledge on the dead? God wants us to utilize it *here*, in *these* physical bodies.

We all say we want to be happy. Do we mean it? Are we even going to give it one real attempt, or do we actually enjoy the misery and suffering here on earth? I say enough is enough, and this is a plea to actually wake up and live the way we were intended to. Don't we all want our individual afterlife experiences to be filled with satisfaction and a sense of accomplishment, knowing that we actually lived in love in all we did and said?

I know that there have been thousands of teachings on walking in love, and this book will explain some of them. We are created by a loving God, no matter whether you are Jewish, Buddhist, Muslim, or Christian. We cannot biologically segregate our death experiences, no matter what version of the story we believe here on earth. The Jesus Christ that I know and love would *not* stand sternly in protest and declare "I am labeled 'Christian' but you are labeled 'Other' so I cannot associate with you." No. The Jesus that I know would embrace everyone regardless of what labels they wore.

> *This is my command: Love each other.*
> — John 15:17 (ERV)

Dr. Long states, "The evidence of near-death experiences points to an afterlife and a universe guided by a vastly loving intelligence." This is the very science that can contribute to peace on earth. We are creating what we now term a global economy in this world. With trade, modern innovations and communication, the Internet, technology, and transportation, we can be anywhere at any time. We openly and freely share in research of all subjects to keep advancing as a human race. However, the differences in our religions seem to be the very things that actually keep us from truly becoming one world. If we really are becoming a global economy, we had better start cooperating with one another, stop fighting, and just look at science. Let science prove the one *truth* that we are all searching for.

So what is God's will? It is love—plain and simple. It is time for the Lord's Prayer to be answered. It is time to live as though heaven is on earth.

So how do we do that? How do we lace love into every facet of our lives in such a way that we live in higher quality? How do we intertwine love into every detail so that we are not thinking of death but rather living "more abundantly," as Jesus put it? Well, I will finally wrap up this introduction to STABLE and provide this philosophy to you as a road map on just how to do that. Three extremely important portions of our lives contribute to a peaceful, joyous, and loving life. STABLE is an acronym that stands for Sound Thought, Always Believe, and Life of Excellence. To summarize, we need to think correctly, believe in our Creator, love Him, and have faith. In our relationships, our choices of words, materialism, reaching our goals, and all else we do, we must do them with love at the core. Over the course of this book, as I discuss these three principles, I will always bring you back to love, which is the universal key to all things. You will understand how to apply these loving principles to all areas of your life. I want each and every one of us to open our hearts and minds to the messages from the afterlife. Let us fully embrace these discoveries wholeheartedly. Let us wrap our arms around this truth, grasp it with all of our strength, pull it back into this life, and let it be our ultimate guide. Let STABLE heal our individual souls and then be used as a tool to bring the entire world together as one.

Then, you will truly understand how to live as though heaven is on earth.

Chapter Two

Sound Thought: The S.T. Principle

You are what you fill your mind with.
— Janice Lewis, my mom

Now that you understand how the STABLE philosophy came to be and what its purpose is, let's dive into it. It is a philosophy or way of life intended to mesh love, in any way that it can, with every detail of your life. The question in each of the three principles that compose STABLE will always be, "What is the key?" and the answer will always bring us back to love. Don't we want life on earth to be as it is in heaven? Yes, we do. We have established that. We are ready to explore the first principle, the S.T. Principle, or Sound Thought. Sound Thought here will be defined as healthy and pleasant thoughts, no matter whether we are thinking about any aspect of ourselves, others, or the world around us.

What is the key to Sound Thought? It is love. What does that mean exactly? And if we know that, scientifically, the nature of God is love, then how do we apply that to

Sound Thought? Near-death experience case studies experienced an overwhelming sense of love and acceptance like they had never felt before, and I might note that quite a few of them knew that they had not lived ideal lives. Many of them had even tried to commit suicide. Yet there was a common occurrence that they felt, the feeling of complete and total acceptance, not just by a loving being but of themselves. I know for a fact, and this is just putting it very mildly and speaking generally, that most of us do *not* accept ourselves. We do not accept our appearances, attributes, talents, financial statuses—and the list goes on. This is what leads to the thoughts in our minds that are *unsound*. We must take a long and serious look at how we think and view ourselves before we can tackle anything else. We have to love ourselves, and others, of course, but it starts from within. I am not talking about a puffed-up conceit and selfishness but a peace like no other with regard to where we are in life, mistakes we have made, our unique gifts and talents, our unique sets of experiences, what we are here to do, the bodies God has given us, and the challenges He has presented before us. It means loving ourselves from an eternal perspective, unconditionally, as God loves us.

I believe that God wants humankind to step things up a notch. We have the resources, and we have been given all of the messages. We have the knowledge and the tools to now advance as a human race, to get past the veil of this world and its falsehoods. We cannot ever fully achieve what the world portrays to us as an acceptable reality. We may find small pieces of it, but we cannot ever have it all. Yet somehow we manage to spin our wheels in search of what the world deems as perfection, like a dog chasing its tail. We are exhausted and exasperated that we cannot ever find the airbrushed fairy tale. We remain blind to the truth that we are here for a much greater purpose than to merely consume and then loathe ourselves when we cannot live up to the world's standards. Mankind is trapped in this vicious cycle and cannot escape without an incredible fight. I believe that God wants us to advance and see His reality, to see ourselves as He sees us.

Inside Out

We attempt to slap on nail polish, wear the right name brands, live in the nicest houses, drive the latest cars, have the latest phones, and so on. I was once one of those people. It is all an illusion that I just could not keep up with. I got tired of the cycle of material decay, the constant letdown when my cars aged, my shoes wore out, the nail polish chipped off, and the perfectly manicured lawn grew weeds. Having said that, I certainly believe in taking pride in our appearance and belongings and even in treating ourselves to earthly gifts. Please do not mistake this. I am saying that we are insatiable and obsessed with having more, more, more. Material goods are just way too high on our list of priorities. That is all. It is like a drug that the world has used to hold and imprison us, yet most worldly people wonder why they are so very, very depressed. There is so much more than this endless and futile cycle of material decay. There is something that truly never dies. That is love. We are here for but the blink of an eye. When I meditate on this fact, it makes the world's falsehoods just fade away, not in a morbid way, but in such a way that causes me to live and love more deeply.

Everything we do is in the opposite direction. We reach outward to grasp and pull everything in toward us and hold on tightly to it, hoping that somehow our lives are going to work. It is time for each and every one of us, young and old alike, to work in the completely opposite direction, to do a 180-degree turn. It is time that we, as a world, look into our own selves and find that peace and acceptance that we are going to feel anyway when we pass from these bodies. When we finally find a healthy acceptance of ourselves, then and only then will we see the natural by-products. When we accept ourselves unconditionally, it is inevitable that we will find greater levels of peace in our families, our communities, and ultimately our world. The whole world is trying to solve problems with the "war on this" and the "war on that." Most of the problems in the world would be solved if people would simply work on their inner selves. Author Ron Martino describes this best in his book *The Self-Image Solution*. He explains that self-love is the answer to relationships, addictions, and more—a type of cutting off the source of the problem rather than placing a bandage over it. He believes that when we humbly love and care for ourselves before all else, all other aspects of our lives are just naturally healthy. We do not wish ill or destruction for ourselves, and fighting earthly temptations becomes easier.

Let me put it into perspective. If we are doing something over and over and it just is not working (i.e., there is still war, drug use, and domestic violence; we are still depressed;

we are still frustrated) in spite of all of the bandages, government programs, and efforts, then *it just is not working*. I would ask that the whole world turn everything upside down and change the way we are all operating because the manner in which we function *is not working*. That is what I am asking each and every person on this planet to do. Instead of attacking issues after the fact, we must truly get to the source, which is our inner selves, first and foremost.

When I started fixing myself on the inside, that is when I found happiness. My best beauty products were a Bible, a treadmill, a good pair of sneakers, some good vitamins, and a self-help book or two. I began to work from the inside out, which was the opposite direction I had been moving throughout my entire life. After I truly realized the nature of God, I developed a peace with myself, with all of my flaws, unpleasant experiences, and tragic errors. Because I finally accepted myself, over time I began to enjoy simple gifts like sunshine, beautiful music, and laughter. I refused to wrestle with what the world painted as perfect. Manmade things do not last. Now that I have fixed the inside of myself, I no longer live the materialistic, vengeful, selfish, angry, and resentful life I once did. I live with the complete acceptance and peace that I will experience when I die anyway. It is complete freedom to live this way now while I am on earth. Things like nail polish, clothes, and cars mean nothing to me now. They are but a treat that I can look at and experience with the knowledge that they are fleeting. They are merely rewards, not taken so seriously, that I can experience with a healthy mind-set, knowing that the nature of God is nothing but good. He wants us to have simple pleasures in our lives. It is not about denying oneself but about creating a realistic perspective of what lasts forever.

Depression: How It Affects Our World

Your eyes will shine, and your heart will thrill with joy. — Is. 60:5 (NLT)

Depression is such a sad and tragic part of life that has spread the world over like a cancer. It causes us to despise ourselves, and it feeds on itself. When we despise ourselves, we cope with drugs and alcohol, we are unkind to others, we verbally and physically abuse strangers and loved ones, we refuse to forgive, and we are bitter and angry. We act out in despair in ways that cause us to lose our families and everything we have ever worked for. Families break down, society breaks down, communities break down, nations break down. Nations battle one another over hate. So you see, however slowly, our own depression ripples out from us like a wave. Collectively, when most of us are depressed, the whole world ultimately feels the ugly effects. Healing ourselves and making this a better world to live in begins at the individual level. Just as depression has a collective effect, so does happiness. It may seem that achieving collective happiness is a daunting task, but all you really need to work on is yourself. Then you watch the positive effects that radiate from you. Depression is wreaking havoc on our world in more ways than we can begin to realize. I went through it for a very, very, long time, and I am truly an example of how an individual's breaking down leads to the family's doing the same. When families break down, so does the community, and so on and so on.

Recently, in a *New York Times* article, the World Health Organization revealed its conclusions on the effects of depression. It stated that depression is the leading cause—yes, I said *leading cause*—of disability and is on track to be the second-leading contributor to global disease by the year 2020. Depression affects everything, including our immune systems, blood pressure, heart health, and more. Prolonged depression has even been found to cause permanent damage to the hippocampus portion of the brain, the area responsible for memory and learning. Depression is a very real and catastrophic epidemic. Havoc and chaos are active in this world, and we must do something about it. *We*, meaning every single person, have to turn the world upside down, turn it around, and start operating in the opposite direction from that which we are accustomed to as a human race because we are destroying ourselves. We are filled with discord and are physically sick because of it. I know that there most certainly are other contributors to disease and disability, but we have the ability to make ourselves healthier, and this is what I want to discuss in the next part of this chapter.

I would like to pause here and express my awareness that these principles and this philosophy will not be accepted by everyone. But the part of me that sees the good in everyone has to believe in the human tendency to want answers, to know God, and to live a better life. You must really want this to make it happen. God made us in His image, and He lives in all of us. There is a love deep down inside of us that must come out and seek our Creator. If you seek Him, you will find Him. I believe that the world is changing and is going to change even more in a significant way. I believe that this is a great start, and soon the world will be filled with a beautiful existence.

So Just How Do We Get Happy?

How does this all apply to the principle of Sound Thought? Well, and I will say this repeatedly, we need to experience while we are here on earth what we will experience after this life. Again, why wait? Let us get it right in one lifetime. Sound Thought involves loving ourselves with the joyous celebration and acceptance that we will feel after this life.

> *For as he thinks in his heart, so is he.*
> — Prov. 23:7 (AMP)

I realize that there is a lot of inspirational material out there. Over many years, I heard phrases like "Think positive thoughts," "Just be happy," and so on. But I just could not wrap my head around these simple concepts, no matter how hard I tried. Even if I had a good day, the upbeat mood would disappear as soon as it arrived. And so I remained defeated and sick with depression. I needed something, anything, to fix me. One day, after much suffering and after the seed of STABLE had been planted, I realized that I needed a play-by-play instruction manual. I had to come up with a very practical and visual approach to healing. I was tired of seeing therapists and rehashing the same problems weekly. Medications left me in a fog. Nothing worked.

So, here is what happened. The day that I recognized the dichotomy and presence of both positive and negative thoughts is the day that I truly healed. When I accepted negative thoughts, I actually found happiness! It is all about deciding which thoughts will get your attention, which ones win you over, and which ones you decide to believe.

> *Our hearts ache, but we always have joy.*
> — 2 Cor. 6:10 (NLT)

I used to believe that I could not heal my depression until there were no more negative thoughts entering my mind about who I was, what I was doing, my abilities, my appearance, and my experiences. I imagined that a magical day would someday arrive on which I would wake up happy and my malaise would be a distant memory. However, it was just another mirage that I was chasing. I would, on occasion, have some happy days in which I was thinking positively about myself and my life, only to wake up and find that the positive thoughts were gone. Done. All of the negativity would come back, and I would grieve over my failure to hold onto my best days. "Oh, my goodness,"

I would say to myself. "Why did these negative thoughts come back? I thought I was doing so well. I guess I just cannot do it." Ultimately, I would brush off all of the 'think positive thoughts' clichés that I heard as an unattainable joke and accept defeat and sadness. I could not, for the life of me, understand why my thoughts of failure, hopelessness, and worthlessness would not go away.

Well, the truth is that they simply won't. Expecting anything other than that is unrealistic. Now, please do not put this book down and think that I am saying you cannot defeat depression. There just came a time when I had to get real. There is a solution that makes this struggle more practical and gives us more confidence in our abilities to beat it for good. So please bear with me as I get to the point.

You can decide which voices in your mind you will listen to. Even when you are in your darkest hour, you can say things that you may not even believe. When I was at my lowest points, I still had the ability to say, "I will get happy. This will pass, and I have a bright future," even with tears rolling down my face. I did not always believe those words, but the more I said them, the more I came to believe them—eventually (and by this, I mean years later). And eventually is certainly better than never.

One of the world's most influential motivational authors is Dr. Deepak Chopra. He too has claimed that he does not believe in positive thinking exclusively, or even at all. He puts a different spin on it, of course, and he teaches creativity, stillness of the mind, and such, which are also wonderful things. However, I am going to put my own spin on positive thinking—I do not believe in 100 percent positive thinking 100 percent of the time. It is not realistic. In these physical bodies and in this world, it is simply not possible. The human race is highly advanced. We have arrived at an unbelievable level of achievement in space exploration, the Internet, and modern medicine, but we do not have complete awareness and control over our own minds … *yet*. It is imperative that we evolve. The mind is a final frontier for us humans because we have shown that we have no problems advancing in all other areas. If only we could master this. If only we could laugh in the face of negativity, no matter how severe. Think of the problems that could be solved. Imagine a world filled with individuals who were masters of their minds and every thought. What would happen? We would be a world that does not give in to addictions, violent behavior, greed, gossip, anger, lust, and so on. In a world filled with people who could conquer their thoughts, the by-product behaviors would result in healthier families, communities, and nations. It starts with the source, the human mind. Social services for domestic abuse, drug treatment programs, wars on crime, guns, drugs, and more are necessary, but let's also declare war on the minds of every single person in this world and just watch what happens.

In recent years, there was a huge media and internet buzz and crazed rumors about the Mayan calendar's ending in 2012, which, according to the interpretations of many, marked the "evolution of consciousness." I wholeheartedly agree. It is absolutely time for us to evolve.

The Dichotomy of Thought

In Chile in 2010, thirty-three miners were trapped nearly half a mile underground for over two months. The harrowing situation made headlines worldwide as no one was quite sure if these men would survive. Their only hope of survival hinged on food transferred to them in tubes for what seemed like forever as the world waited on the edge of its seat to learn of their fate. In October 2010, all of them were miraculously rescued, an awesome event that inspired the entire world. One of the rescued miners emotionally stated after his rescue, "I was with God, and I was with the devil. They fought, and *God won!*" I bring this story to your attention because it perfectly summarizes the Sound Thought Principle. You can hear the positive and you can hear the negative. *Let the positive win!*

Many of us go to school so we can do what we want to do. If you want to be a lawyer, you go to law school. If you want to be a doctor, you go to medical school. If you want to be a dental assistant, you go to school. Even if you want to be a yoga instructor, you go to school. It's a pretty simple and basic concept, right? You would think so. However, the whole hurting world is so desperate to be happy. So why, oh, why—as we wake up every stinking morning saying to ourselves, *What's wrong with me? Why do I feel this way? Why can't I just be happy? I am so tired of living this way!*—why can't we just go to a school of sorts? Let us learn and train ourselves daily, once and for all, on how to be happy. If I want to be a teacher, I certainly cannot pop a magic pill or vent to someone weekly about how much I want to be a teacher and expect that desire to be fulfilled.

If I only do those things, I will never be a teacher! So why is learning how to be happy any different?

If we want to be happy, we should be studying it and practicing it every day. It should be a part of our daily agenda, like brushing our teeth. It should be the first thing we think about when we wake up in the morning. Our minds and emotions need not be like torn plastic bags, blowing about randomly in the wind. We are to hold and maneuver the strings that control the puppet that is our minds. I personally used to become very tired of seeing peace signs and "Be happy" messages everywhere from bumper stickers to T-shirts unless I could live it myself. Happiness is not a myth like the Loch Ness Monster or Bigfoot that people talk about but never actually see or experience. It is real. The joy discovered in the afterlife is God's intention for us now, not when are lives on earth come to an end. It is time for the curtain to come down and reveal what we have allowed to be hidden away from us but has been available to us all along.

We let our thoughts run all over us, and we accept them as part of who we are, as if we are completely blind and at their mercy. *I'm never going to amount to anything. I've made too many mistakes in my life. It's too late for me. I don't look like that supermodel in the magazine. She told me my ankles were too large. He said that my talents were a joke.* Our thoughts are either recordings that play relentlessly the things others have told us in our lifetimes, or they are twisted and contorted because we feel that, somehow, we do not conform to the world's standards. Regardless of the source of the thoughts, we let them defeat and crush us.

We neglect to see ourselves as perfect and unique pieces of God's plan.

> *He chose to give birth to us by giving us His true word. And we, out of all creation, became His prized possession.* — James 1:18 (NLT)

Thoughts can ruin our lives. Napoleon Hill was a great inspirational figure of the early 1900s. His philosophies stated simply that "thoughts become things." In other words, negative thoughts are able to transform into revenge, hurtful words, drug and alcohol addictions, divorce, violence, and more. This is a cycle that continues from generation to generation. When will we end this cycle of madness? Are we doomed as a race to act poorly, complain, act poorly, complain, act poorly, complain … on and on until the end of time? No. There is a happy ending. God knows we have already won. God knows that we will change.

> *And God will wipe every tear from their eyes.*
> — Rev. 7:17 (NLT)

In my children's school and in schools across America, there is a new awareness of bullying. The new antibullying campaign is absolutely wonderful in that it teaches kids to be kind to others and respect diversity. It teaches them character and makes them aware of the damage that words can cause. The campaign, however, may be missing a crucial piece of the puzzle. Often, it does not first address the *source* before the bullying even happens; our own minds are the biggest bullies of all. It certainly is a wonderful thing when children learn not to mistreat other people, but they need to learn not to mistreat themselves first. It is the children who are uncomfortable with themselves and are hurting inside that lash out at other children the most. This is a key element that must be added to this fierce and fantastic campaign. The bullying problem will never be eliminated unless children's minds and ways of thinking about themselves are corrected and made healthy. The campaign can also serve largely as a preventative measure rather than a bandage. As parents, we can serve as examples when we also possess a healthy self-esteem. Schools can add to the antibullying initiative a variety of ways that kids can fight negativity in all of its forms. I know firsthand that the times in my life when I have hurt the most inside and my mind has completely taken me over are when I have hurt people in my life beyond repair. Kids are no different, and this remains true for all of us. I must admit that I have witnessed bullying as an adult just as much, if not more, as I did in my childhood. The antibullying campaign must extend beyond school-age children and to adult work environments and our communities. We are our own biggest bullies. Let us fix how we are all thinking individually first.

So the question you are most likely asking is, "Okay, so how do I do that?" Peace, joy, and happiness all sound great, but we all need directions or an actual how-to demonstration. I, like many of you, had not one single clue about how to be a happy person. I just knew I wanted it more than anything. We may not even be aware that we are miserable because it is often accepted as a natural way of life. We are so used to it that we would not feel "normal" being happy for the better portion of our lives. Perhaps we would feel a lack of control without constant fear and worry over every detail of our lives. However, it is possible. And we will adjust.

Being happy must be defined here. You must forget everything that you think happiness is. Remember, I am trying to move you away from the world's standards. *Happiness* means finding peace in everything and every circumstance. I will confess to you that as I am writing this, I have very little money. I have less than $100 in the bank, and I have a $20 bill in my purse. I am not sure how I will financially manage this month. But I can say with all honesty that I have never been happier in my life. My lack of material things has redirected me to find happiness in the fresh flowers in my yard, the sunny breeze that is outside, the birds that provide beautiful music, and the laughter of my children. These are all things that I did not consider with their due priority when my resources were once endless and I drove a Mercedes. *Happiness* means taking positive action with confidence and getting results, which are things that fear, worry, and negative thinking will never accomplish. Complaining and moaning are fruitless; they are not real but imagined control and are needed only if we really want our problems to continue as they exhaust our useful energy. Happiness also lies in the awareness of an afterlife, as it will someday offer us a feeling of incredible joy. That constant awareness of my final destination melts away all of the pettiness of this world that I once took all too seriously. It is a method of living that does not separate my life 'here' and my life 'there', but rather a blending of two very real worlds into one. This awareness of what is to come makes me enjoy the simple beauties of this life all the more.

So here is what I did: I had to start thinking of my brain and its detrimental thoughts as a collective bully, as a separate entity from myself. I had to talk to it, get angry with it, and tell it to stop. Many times I could be seen and heard talking out loud to it. I am quite sure that many a person next to me at many a red light wasn't sure if I was on a hands-free phone call or just speaking to myself. This was my "school," the daily habit that I utilized to graduate into happiness. It was a practice that lasted for years. It would not and could not happen in a day, week, or month. I was fiercely determined to brainwash myself into bliss. Finally, I was able to push against this force in my mind with an even greater force and dominate.

The Strangers at the Door

I need to use a hypothetical scenario to help you visualize and understand just how to approach domination over negativity. Let us pretend that it is a very cold Saturday morning at six o'clock. You are sound asleep and quite cozy in your warm bed. It is your day off after a long week of work, and you can sleep in as long as you would like. Suddenly, you hear loud and persistent banging at the front door. The doorbell rings frantically and repeatedly. You peel your eyes open and drag yourself out of bed and to the front door wondering what could possibly be so urgent at this early hour. You open the door, and standing in front of you is a large and intimidating person (you provide the visual). This individual forces his or her way into your home, practically knocking you over. He or she points a crooked finger in your face and begins to yell very loudly. With a berating tone, this person proceeds to inform you at this early hour that you will never amount to anything. "Why try? Why bother?" he or she shouts. Then the person reminds you of that huge mistake that you made that cost you your financial security or a relationship or both, that you are too overweight, that you will never change, that you are not like your neighbor down the street and never will be, that you will never get over what a certain person did to you, that the world is just crushing you, and that your dreams and visions are silly. "Who do you even think you are, thinking you could ever reach that goal? You might as well just give up. You are so depressed, and that is how you always will be—paralyzingly and morbidly depressed. This is your life. You are hopeless."

I know this is a ridiculous scenario, and chances are good that it will never happen to you. But if you think about it, this is pretty much what happens to most of us before we even get out of bed. That stranger at the door, my friend, is the thoughts in your own mind.

Yes, it is very unlikely that someone would go out of his way to scream at some randomly selected person. But let us just imagine that it really did happen to you. What would you do? How would you react? Please think about this for a moment. Personally, I would not hesitate to tell this intimidating person to leave, forcefully push him or her out of my home, and call the police or even 9-1-1. While doing all of this, I would be doing a lot of screaming and yelling right back at them. I may even react by shouting, "Who are you? Get out of my house! I am not listening to this! Are you crazy? Get out!"

To really drive my point home, I would like to flip the coin for a moment. I want to offer you an even more ridiculous scenario—more ridiculous because it is even less likely to happen than the first. Let us just say, hypothetically, that the same large and looming individual goes about the same type of verbal home invasion, showing up at your door at sunrise on a Saturday morning and shouting the same insults right in your face. This time, however, you react quite differently. This time, you invite the bully into your home. You timidly reply, "Here, have a seat on the sofa. Let me make you a cup of coffee. You can stay, can't you? Please tell me more. I want to hear what you have to say." After listening to him or her yammer on about your many alleged faults, you whimper, "Really? Do you really think so? Oh, I guess you must be right. Well, now I am really depressed. But that is what you say, so it's true. That really is who I am." The stranger leaves feeling very satisfied. You crawl back into your bed, pull the covers over your head, and give up.

I hope I have made my point and you realize just how silly that scene is. No one in a right frame of mind would treat a verbally abusive home invader off the street with such welcoming warmth—*no one*. So why do we accept the degrading thoughts in our own brains, as they are nothing more than that metaphorical stranger?

I remember sitting in my car with dark, horrible thoughts running over and over through my mind, like, *I have made too many mistakes, and now I have to start my life all over again. I am never going to be able to recover from all that I have lost. No one will want me. No one loves me. I am a horrible person with no gifts or abilities. I am too old to start again. It is too late for me. I will always be broke. My skin is a mess—too many pimples, too many wrinkles. My ankles are too big. I am too short. I will never amount to anything so I might as well plan my suicide.* Truthfully, that was the state of my mind, and I could not see above it, around it, or through it. It was what I thought. Therefore, it was who I was.

However, I also recall sitting in that same car with the same thoughts months later, and I began to talk to them as I would any cruel stranger. I exclaimed out loud, "No! Be quiet! That is not true! You are wrong!" I would blurt out these responses anywhere that I was—in the grocery store or walking down the street. I am sure people thought either that I was on the phone or that I was just plain crazy. But I had to treat this just like I would a bully at my front door. I had to practice it not for days, not for weeks, and not for months. I had to practice it for years until that stranger at the door went away or, at times, hid in the corner, hoping for my attention.

Let us recognize both the positive and the negative.

Conversely, there may be another stranger at your door, again, bright and early on a Saturday when you are quite sound asleep. However, when you answer the door this time, you are welcomed by the most pleasant, angelic, and warm individual. This kind stranger proceeds to tell you, "No matter how long it takes, with discipline and baby steps, you will reach your goals. It does not matter how old you are. It is never too late. You can beat your addictions. You can improve your relationship with your spouse. You have gifts from God that are unique and unlike any others', and He will help you to use them. You are one of a kind. You may not look like the man-made ideal in magazine photos, but those are not the truth, anyway. God created you for a purpose, and you are beautiful and fully accepted in His eyes." Upon hearing this, you completely accept and love yourself the same way that God loves you.

I certainly would (and I know you would too) be more inclined to invite this particular stranger into my home and offer him or her a cup of coffee. I would sit this person down on my sofa and ask to hear more. I would prefer to pay attention to this Good Samaritan. And I ask you again, how are your own brain and random thoughts any different? They are not.

See God, who is positive; see the devil, the negative, the accuser. But make a commitment that no matter how clouded your mind becomes, you will believe God and God alone, no matter what. Say it repeatedly even if you do not believe it at first. Eventually you will.

I was at peace with myself. Nothing hurt. I could only see my life and self through that Being's Love.

> *There was no negative in myself or from that Being*
> *for anything I had done.*
>> — One near-death account recorded
>> in *Evidence of the Afterlife*

Another metaphoric scenario is that *both* of these strangers, the bully and the kind soul, have made their way into your home and have *both* planted themselves on your sofa. One is filling your ears with the truth of the gifts and positive attributes you possess, and the other tells you the lie that you are worthless and so on. *You now have the ability in your anger over this argument to tell one of them that he or she is a liar and that the other is telling the truth.* If you have the ability to speak to two strangers who are in *your* home, then how is it that you completely lose the ability to speak to your own mind and random thoughts? There is no reason you cannot—no reason at all.

Just watch what happens if you practice this every single day, for years if you have to. You can bet that the stranger who came into your home and is bullying you and pushing you around will get tired and bored and feel ignored when he or she discovers that no one is really listening to him or her, or even taking him or her seriously. The bully may decide to go off into the corner when it is no longer the center of attention or may even leave your home altogether. Now here is the catch ... *he or she will always return.* The sooner you accept this, the better. Just be ready for it.

I practiced this technique of treating my own thoughts like other people, and when the bully inevitably returned, with each new visit it became more and more of a joke. Even when it had me in an absolute headlock, I always knew it would eventually leave. And so I accepted this as the ebb and flow of my life. I found true happiness knowing that this hostile visitor did not speak the truth. I could laugh at it. It would leave and return again and again. Each time, one of my favorite things to say out loud was, "Nice try!"

I strive to put these tactics into very simple terms because depression is so complex. In a nutshell, that is how I healed. That is how I got happy. And you can too.

> *When my enemies and foes attack me, they will stumble and fall. Though a mighty army surrounds me, my heart will not be afraid. Even if I am attacked, I will remain confident.*
>
> — Ps. 27:2–3 (NLT)

We are all unique individuals with a God-given plan for our lives. Later chapters will discuss this in more depth. However, we need to accept ourselves the way God accepts us. I used to hear people say, "God loves you" or "God is love," but I did not really understand exactly what that meant. I was one of those people who believed it because it was what I had been taught and what I was supposed to believe. Not only has God transformed my life and shown me His love for me, but the scientific study of near-death experiences has validated for me all that I have ever learned about the nature of God. Through my experience with God, all He has shown me about myself, and all the unexpected blessings and wonder He has bestowed upon me, I have come to love Him with a peace and joy that I never could have expected.

This principle of listening to and believing only one voice in our minds applies not only to what we think of ourselves physically but also to our abilities and capabilities to achieve our goals, and even our relationships. Guilt, shame, and fear are three of the biggest obstacles to achieving anything, especially thinking in a healthy, positive, Godlike fashion. Guilt, shame, and fear can cause sinking paralysis. We freeze as time and life march on, unable to make a move or a single decision. These can be the hardest thought patterns to break free from. What I came to realize after wallowing in my own guilt, shame, and fear after failing at so many things in my life, from finances to relationships to a career, is that these three things are also some of the greatest forms of selfishness.

You may fail at anything. For example, you may lose your job, your marriage may fall apart, you may make a life-changing mistake, or you may resume your addiction once again. Everyone around you suffers when you fail, and somehow you feel as though you may be more worthy of forgiveness or even vindicated if you have a pity party for the rest of your life so that neither you nor anyone around you can forget about your transgression. We feel, for some reason, that if we punish ourselves forever in a pit of despair, our loved ones will feel better knowing how much regret and remorse we have. We fear that if we actually pick ourselves up, brush off the dirt, hold our chins up, and march forward without looking back, our loved ones will think we are not deeply sorry. This could not be farther from the truth. What God and everyone else around us really wants is for us to be examples of strength, to admit our mistakes to God and the ones we love, to stand up straight, and to persevere with a smile, knowing that God has forgiven us and that He still has work for us to do. Do not let your life become a tragedy in which one grave error steals the gift of life from you for all eternity.

You never thought of anyone else; you just saw your pain. — Kelly Clarkson

The principle of Sound Thought is needed more than ever when we are experiencing guilt, shame, or fear. The Bible says in Ecclesiastes 7:20 (NLT), "Not a single person on earth is always good and never sins." And 1 John 3:20 (NLT) says, "Even if we feel guilty God is greater than our feelings." God is *greater* than the thoughts that tell us we are no good and never will be because of the mistakes we have made. Guilt is also a sign that we care. It can be deeply sorrowful knowing that we have hurt another or even changed the course of someone's life in some way. If you are feeling guilt, please acknowledge that it is a form of sorrow and remorse and an awareness that you desperately want to avoid repeating your mistake. Allow yourself even the smallest amount of modest and humble credit for this and move on. The Bible explains to us that what the devil intends for evil, God has intended for good. Get out of the rut of despair and paralyzing sorrow over what you have done. If you have to suffer, gosh darn it, at least let something good come from it! Do not let it go to waste! Do not let it be for nothing! You have the ability to help another with the lessons you have learned. I once heard it put like this: "Do not hog your experiences." God can use the most tragic things in life and turn them into beautiful and wonderful works.

Too many of us give up on things too quickly. But as I said before, if we really want to be doctors, we have no problem investing years in schooling. Do not give up on finding happiness.

I practiced Sound Thought for years, and I finally got it. No longer did I believe the lies in my mind, no matter how tight their grip on me was or how they originated. Even to the present day, I must still utilize Sound Thought. Sometimes negativity's grip on me is so strong that it is all I can do to muster a weak and brief little protest. I know with my entire mind, body, and heart what the truth about myself really is. I know the *truth*, which is what God thinks of me. As I said earlier, I will keep returning to the nature of God, which is love and acceptance. I want to live as though heaven is on earth. I want you to also. In every little thing I do, say, and think, I want to reflect that day when I meet my Creator. I want to have no regrets. I want to know what is expected of me now and do it while I have the chance. So I must look to discoveries of the afterlife to be my guide.

Let love be the key to Sound Thought, that love that we all experience when we leave this earth. Make it heaven on earth. Love and accept yourself *now.*

The Media

We are surrounded by a media illusion everywhere we go, one that is man-made and that we can never obtain. We see false images of pristine homes; unblemished skin; long legs; lean, airbrushed bodies; couples who do not quarrel; and the list goes on. Somewhere, somehow, very recently in this world's very long history, someone decided what perfection is and made us slaves to the never-ending and unrealistic feat of obtaining it, leading us to live our lives like hamsters in a wheel, exhausted and getting nowhere. Occasionally, we are able to stop and enjoy a brief oasis that will soon fade or be replaced by yet a new and improved oasis that we must now keep expending our resources and energy to reach. So many of us repeat this process throughout our entire lives and never understand why we are always frustrated and exhausted and have nothing but insecurities about ourselves, tattered relationships, and bitterness in our hearts as we give undeserved priority to earthly endeavors.

I will never look like Heidi Klum nor even have legs as long as hers no matter how many items I purchase from Victoria's Secret. Of course, she is an absolutely beautiful woman, but who said her type of body is an ideal? Who said? I implore you not to buy into this man-made view of "perfection." It is simply not attainable or possible. Even if only a glimpse of it is realized, it will most certainly decay and fade away.

> *Those who love money will never have enough. How meaningless to think that wealth brings true happiness! —* Ecc. 5:10 (NLT)

People who have reported near-death experiences have never once recalled dissatisfaction over not driving the latest car, having the latest phone, wearing the latest fashions, or having a certain pant size. Their experiences are based only on things that last forever—relationships, how we treat others, and love. That is all.

I certainly am not saying that God does not want us to enjoy this life; He absolutely does. I most certainly enjoy new clothes, eating at restaurants, and buying home décor. But when we strip away the material and the unessential, we have enjoyment. Even the great martial artist Bruce Lee expressed that, in terms of material things, life is about decrease, not increase. We have communities of which we can be a part; we have families we can adore; and we have the warm sunshine, the beautiful and bright colors of flowers, and the relaxation of a cool rain. We have laughter, affection, and kind words to hear and speak. We have beloved possessions that can be re-used or recycled or repaired, and do not require constant replacement. We can decorate our homes with leaves, branches, and found objects from nature- for free! The best days of my life have been filled with those things and those things alone.

Surely I have felt the excitement of shopping or buying new things. But I look around in my attic and find many of those things—old shoes that once "made my day" but that I no longer give a waking thought to, for example. Maybe this realization comes only with age and experience, the realization of the cycle of highs and lows that material items can bring. But if this message can touch the mind and heart of a young person who can learn this valuable lesson now, then I have done my job. If I can alter the life of a middle-aged or seasoned person who needs a change in perspective, then I have succeeded.

Enjoy your life. Treat yourself. But place love above all else. Do not be brainwashed by the world.

The Sound Thought Principle to See the Best in Others

If a man truly be great he will be compassionate, sympathetic, and tolerant. He will love the good and bad among all humanity. The good he will love with pride and admiration and joy. The bad he will love with pity and sorrow, for he will know, if he truly be great, that both good and bad qualities in men often are but the results of circumstances over which they have... little control. The great minds of every age have recognized love as the eternal elixir that binds the heartwounds of mankind and makes men their brothers' keepers. If a man truly be great, he will love all mankind! — Napoleon Hill

The Sound Thought Principle applies not only to discovering the best qualities in ourselves but also to finding the best of qualities in others. The thoughts that we allow to win over our minds regarding others ultimately affect how we treat them and speak to them. You can choose the proper thoughts, which turn into kinder words and actions. You can use the "stranger at the door" tactic to believe the best of your spouse, your coworkers, and your friends. What begins to happen then is magical. When we believe the best about our loved ones, it manifests itself in our words and actions toward them. It encourages them. It creates an incentive and morale for them to flourish, and it is contagious. It returns to you in unexpected ways. So you see how gaining this control over your mind can begin to blossom and take over every aspect of your life, with beautiful results.

This is never to suggest that we are not to remove ourselves from damaging situations. We must be safe, first of all. However, within our close relationships, our encounters with strangers, and even our views of humankind on the other side of the globe, we are to love humankind.

> *Love does not dishonor others; it is not self-seeking, it is not easily angered, it keeps no record of wrongs.*
> — 1 Cor. 13:5 (NIV)

The negative in my mind, for example, may want me to moan and groan about the fact that my husband forgot to take out the garbage this week, and last week. This, in turn, may translate into words and actions that hurt and berate him. The *positive* in my mind wants me to acknowledge the fact that he works over sixty hours per week so my family can have what we need and to gently remind him of his simple forgetfulness while offering him understanding about his exhaustion. No one is perfect. I most certainly am not. It is just garbage we are talking about here. God is not concerned about the trash in my garage, but He is interested in how I treat my spouse. This, of course, is only one example of millions of similar scenarios. Way too many times in my life have I acted,—lashed out, even—on negative, insecure feelings and thoughts of myself as well as fleeting negative thoughts of a loved one. This caused chaos and damage in my path as I gave into these thought processes, only to look around in horror and shock when the dust had settled and the detrimental negativity in my mind finally eased up. What I was left with was loss and tragedy. My advice is to hold on tight and ride negative, angry, and bitter thoughts out like a rough ride. Fight them tooth and nail for they are not worth the incredible damage that they can cause. They come and go like the rain. Do not allow them to sweep away all that really matters to you in your life—a friend, a spouse, a parent.

See people as good and beautiful, even when they seem to be trying hard not to appear so.
— Leo F. Buscaglia, PhD, *Loving Each Other: The Challenge of Human Relationships*

On Conquering Addictions

The same principle may be used when you doubt your ability to give up an addiction that is tearing your life and loved ones apart. Choose to believe the voice in your head that says you will do it! The voice that says you simply cannot have victory over drugs, alcohol, or any other form of addiction is lying to you. Get angry at that lying voice! Get mad! No one likes to be lied to. Enough is enough. Be a warrior! When something pushes against you, push against it with a force that is even greater. If the walls were literally closing in on you, I can guarantee that you would not let yourself be crushed by them. You would push them away from you with all of your strength and might. The thoughts that bombard you day and night are no different.

We are stubborn, we humans. In so many situations, we simply refuse to give in on what we deem as principle. Why, then, do we give into our negative thoughts so very easily? We are entirely too advanced as a human race in all that we have achieved to allow ourselves to remain in such a primordial and archaic way of thinking with no mind or thought control.

So you see, practicing and utilizing the Sound Thought Principle in everything we do creates a healthy image of ourselves, but when we have the same love and respect for ourselves as God has for us, we are no longer miserable. We are free. We build a shield of God's love around us that no negative thought about ourselves or others can penetrate. It builds on itself. It grows and blossoms into a life of healthy relationships at work and home, kind behaviors, more successes, and fewer tragedies as we no longer give into violence and addictions. It blossoms in our families, it catches on in our communities, it grows in our states and nations, and it flows like a wave into the whole world. We begin to experience heaven on earth. It has to begin with each and every individual in all races, genders, ages, and cultures.

With God as our Father, brothers all are we.
Let me walk with my brother, in perfect harmony.
Let peace begin with me, let this be the moment now.
With every breath I take, let this be my solemn vow.
— "Let There Be Peace on Earth and Let It Begin with Me," a song by Jill Jackson and Sy Miller

Isaiah 55:8 (NLT) speaks of God's thoughts. Please think of this in terms of how your mind may be working right now and know this: "My thoughts are nothing like your thoughts. And God's ways are far beyond anything you can imagine." That is the truth.

The Sound Thought Principle for Our Healthy Bodies

Love is the only key to heaven on earth in all of the three principles discussed in this book. Just as we look at the scientific discovery of near-death experiences to understand the nature of God, we can also look at science to validate the principle of Sound Thought itself. Scientists have discovered that our human bodies were engineered to think and behave in positive ways for optimum health. Ecclesiastes 11:10 (NLT) says, "Refuse to worry and keep your body healthy." This was written such a long time ago, without the support of science and advanced study of the human body, but it was undoubtedly right on the mark. God intended for us to choose and live with a positive mind-set.

Dr. Caroline Leaf, researcher and author of *Who Switched Off My Brain?*, has studied the human brain since 1981. In her book, she elaborates on the scientific findings of negative and positive thought processes and their individual effects on the body. Specifically, she has found that negative thought processes in our minds reveal a tree-like image with thorny branches filled with toxic chemicals that burst and are released into our bodies, wreaking havoc and eventually making us ill or resulting in disease. Her book explains, "Researchers say that 87% of the illnesses that plague us today are a direct result of our thought life.... What we think about affects us physically.... It's an epidemic of toxic emotions." Conversely, positive thought processes do not reveal these toxic thorns, or pockets of harmful chemicals, if you will, but rather reward your body with healthy chemicals. Dr. Leaf goes on to explain that these positive thought processes are defined as anything from affirmative views of one's self, love, gratitude, confidence, courageousness, affection, laughter, kindness, forgiveness, prayer, or faith. Doesn't that sound quite like a description of the afterlife as reported by a near-death experience case study? Of course, various levels of pain and illness will be unavoidable as we are human and not immortal. However,

God wants us to live better lives here on earth, and our minds are where it all begins. He designed, engineered, and created our physical bodies to live out the characteristics of heaven in order to have optimum well-being now.

I recall, as a graduate student studying psychology, coming across many clinically written medical journals based on the idea that positive thoughts, benevolence, and forgiveness are healthy for our bodies. This is widely known and recognized in the medical field. Researchers now understand the physical and chemical link between the mind and the body. Any form of negativity, such as low self-esteem, bitterness, or anger, fills your body with poison. Simply put, our minds and our thoughts are connected to our health, literally. So when the World Health Organization states that in 2020, depression is going to be in second place as a leading contributor to the global burden of disability and disease, let us apply a long, hard, and dramatic approach to our thought processes before placing bandages on the irrevocable damage that they cause. Let us undo what we are doing. This is a plea for radical change. Refuse, refuse, refuse to give into these thoughts that can literally destroy your life. *Refuse!* Let evil or the devil try every time and never, never win.

> *Devils cannot defeat me. People cannot disillusion me. Weather cannot weary me. Sickness cannot stop me. Battles cannot beat me. Money cannot buy me ... and hell cannot handle me.*
> — B. J. Morbitzer

As a young Christian, I do not think that I fully grasped what Jesus's messages were truly about. I somehow thought that He was somewhat of a mystical figure who spoke in encouraging parables. He was like a magic wand; if I revered Him, I would someday go to heaven, like a beautiful fairy tale. I now realize that He was teaching us the most practical, beneficial, and even scientific lessons. Somehow, scientists, philosophers, motivational speakers, and the like have gained credit in our modern world for many of Jesus's original teachings, and most, though not all, have falsely heralded them as their own new ideas. Today's researchers are to be honored and appreciated, yes. But we need not disregard Jesus Christ simply because He walked this earth long ago. His example is more relevant to our lives today than ever. He may not have explained things as clinically as a textbook or medical journal on forgiveness would, but folks, the message is the same. Jesus was the psychologist and the motivational speaker, for all intents and purposes. In John 14:6 (NLT) when Jesus humbly stated, "I am the way, the truth, and the life," my goodness, He was right. He was trying to say, if I may paraphrase, that if you follow His ways and apply His teachings in the most practical sense to your life now—loving, forgiving, treating others kindly, and so on—*you will have peace, life, healthy life.* Jesus understood the physical benefits of heavenly behaviors. This is the truth, and today's discoveries have only backed Him up and reinforced His lessons.

Final Thoughts on Sound Thought

Some of us are so addicted to depression. We do not even know who we are unless we are down in the dumps. It is sickening and tragic. We are living in the opposite fashion of how our bodies were engineered to thrive. It is time, again I will say, to live as though heaven is here on earth and have Sound Thought in our minds. Let love be the key in all you do and think. "Love your neighbor as yourself" Mark 12:31 (NIV)

Prayer for Sound Thought

God, surround me with your protection daily. Cleanse my mind of all negativity. May all harmful thoughts leave my mind, and may I choose to see myself as only you see me. May I also choose to see others how you see them. Help me, Lord. I want to live in the health, joy, and peace that you intend for me. Show me how you want me to think and therefore act in all that I say and do. Let a better way of living result from all of this and spill over into every aspect of my life—my confidence, my family, my career ... everything. Help me for as long as it takes, a lifetime even. I know that you will never leave me nor forsake me. Transform my mind according to your ways, not mine. Amen.

Chapter Three

Always Believe: The A.B. Principle

The A.B., or Always Believe, Principle is the second part of STABLE. "Always believe" is a very general statement, of course, and I trust you will benefit from this broad concept if I break it down for you into two parts. The first part I want to address concerning belief is the very simple question, "Do you believe in God, a creator, a loving intelligence that designed you, or do you not?" The fact is that there are many atheists in this world, individuals who believe that we are a biological accident not designed or created by any type of intelligence, and that we cease to exist upon physical death. Furthermore, many who label themselves as part of a religion still struggle with questions and doubt. This will be addressed more later in this chapter. Once you can get beyond this question of the existence of God and are provided with enough basic common sense with which you can now believe in His existence, the next part of the question is, "Do you have faith?" Stretching even further, "Do you have unbelievable, unwavering, and radical faith?" which is really how we need to be living. It is my goal to start you out on a journey of faith in this chapter; in the beginning you may be riddled with doubt, but by the end you will be able to see God and the afterlife as real. I want you to come to a point at which you communicate with God as you would a friend and are aware of His responses. That is where I am in my life, and it has been a most incredible voyage.

You will find that all of the principles in this book build on one another. For example, as you focus on and practice the Sound Thought Principle and you master it over a long period of time (don't forget, it may take years), you can apply it to A.B., the Always Believe Principle, or your faith. In other words, when your mind becomes clouded and overrun with doubt or unbelief in God, you can treat that doubt like the horrible stranger at your door. You can refuse to give in, regardless of how you feel. You can say, "Nice try. No matter what, I believe. I believe in my God, and no matter how I feel, He has a plan and a purpose for me and my life, even amid my troubling circumstances. I will find that purpose, even if I do not understand until I leave this earth." The Bible says that if we resist the devil, he will flee. Resist, resist, resist. Resist it as you would a rude, interrupting intruder.

We are all capable of doubt, unbelief, and wavering faith. I have heard it said that even Mother Teresa had moments of doubt. It cannot be avoided. The brutal truth is that we are all here but for a short time, that death is a reality, and that life is filled with troubles. We all fight tooth and nail for perfection and trouble-free lives, neither of which are attainable. So why do we let this unavoidable imperfection make us doubt God when that imperfection is really just the way of the world? We must create a new mind-set in which we see the world as imperfect and acknowledge the perfection of where we came from and where we are going. It is a realistic approach to life that helps us to lighten up a bit and not get so frustrated when we cannot achieve perfection here.

So, let us address basic belief first. Do you believe in God, or don't you? Let me begin the exploration of this question by sharing a childhood memory. When I was a child, as far back as five years old, I was quite occupied with the question, "What if there was nothing at all?" When I thought about this idea or questioned my parents about it, I became extremely fearful, disturbed even. I can still remember the stark blackness and darkness that would pervade my mind. Even then, I would become even more disturbed at the idea that if nothing at all existed, then there would not even be the black darkness. It was quite difficult for me to wrap my small mind around this very large and looming concept. I certainly did not understand why I was thinking about it at the time, and I do find it ironic that, even at the age of forty, I am more passionate about this notion than ever. I am passionate about it because I am fighting to prove to, to convince, atheists and unbelievers that "nothing" does not exist. The "nothing" I am referring to is the atheistic belief held by many people that nothing is beyond this life—the belief that we humans came from nothing at all, the belief of randomness with no purpose, no control, no plan ... that all is the result of an accidental miracle, if you will.

Some believe that something can arise from nothing, that chemistry in the universe eventually evolved into DNA.

It is absurdity. That makes about as much sense as my computer existing having never been created by anyone and eventually using letters to form this book on its own with no mind or intelligence behind it all. It is impossible. It is common sense that this is just not the case.

Let me add another analogy to help you realize the ridiculousness of atheism. There is a doorknob on the door that I look at as I sit in my office typing this book. As I look at it, I am reminded of the fact that it is not alive. It does not have a mind or intelligence. It has only elemental structure, chemistry, and various metallic and chemical components. I know for a fact that it could sit here on earth for over one million years and *never* be able to create anything, except perhaps breakdown and decay. It could not suddenly develop a mind or evolve into a language—and especially nothing as complex as DNA—that could create the miracles of the human body, a newborn baby, ecosystems that work together in harmony, photosynthesis of plants, or the beauty of the world around us. DNA is information, instruction, made of just a few simple components, and yet the way the components are spelled out determines the miracle that they will create. It is an encoded expression that is essential to all living things. How can we, for one moment, believe that a mind or form of intelligence was not behind it all? Anyone who has ever studied simple high school biology understands the most basic workings of the human mind, which is a thousand or more times more advanced than today's personal computer; the complexities and perfect processes of our digestive systems; and the beautiful formation of a newborn child in its mother's womb. Even these basic understandings make it impossible to believe that a mind did not create them, as they work in such a perfectly planned fashion.

Could a rock create something as beautiful as this universe? Could "nothing at all" create the human body? Atheists seem to have this belief that the truth is either a scientific explanation of an accident or a false myth that the world calls religion. I will fight for the truth with all my might so long as there is breath in me. The views on this topic need not be so polarized. There doesn't have to be such extreme opposition. Again, I will use the most basic analogy and state that just because a car mechanic figures out exactly how a car works does not mean that there was no intelligent mind back in the corporate headquarters that designed the car. The car mechanic does not now possess the authority to claim credit and disregard its creator or even to go as far as to say that the car just showed up out of nowhere all because he now knows and fully understands the car's functions and mechanics. Anyone who publicly made the claim that such incredible technologies such as the personal computer, the Internet, or even the iPhone, "gosh darnit, just done showed up outta nowhere" [ignorance added for effect] and discounted the existence of Bill Gates or Steve Jobs would be the laughing stock of the world. So I am not sure why the universe and all of its amazing qualities should be treated any differently. Atheistic scientists are quite intelligent and have provided the world with incredible knowledge of how biological systems, nature, and the universe work and function. But it stops there. They do not have the credentials to disregard the Creator just because they have discovered how and what God has designed. There is a combined answer to this basic question of where we came from. We were created by an amazing and loving intelligence, and we are advancing enough as humans to understand only a miniscule part of how it was done.

Many noteworthy scientists today have decided to speak their hearts and minds very openly in that they put their hands up in surrender, saying to their critics that they simply cannot explain how life would come from nonlife and have further explained that they just do not want to believe in God. So they take their stance as atheists and fruitlessly hope that, someday, they can explain it. They really are doing us believers a favor because the more they discover about the miraculous workings of the universe, the harder it becomes to justify the belief that an intelligent mind did not create it. The smartest people in the world are *not* those such as Stephen Hawking and the like. The most intelligent people in the world know that they know very little, next to nothing even, and their minds and hearts are open to all that we do not fully understand. It is that type of mind that is true genius.

We are a highly intelligent human race. We have incredible knowledge today in all facets of life. However, where we fall short is our complete and utter segregation of philosophies and facts. We must come to a new level of advancement in all that we now know, meshing truths together into a large picture and creating a combination of theories that explain the whole story. We are not so dumb that we must be ignorant and stubborn and compartmentalize each school of thought to the point that we battle one another over them. Some of us act like kindergarteners on a playground. Let us use love as the key to all, even the age-old question of "Where do we come from?" Let us look at the studies of the near-death experiences and pour them into one pot of theory. Somehow, in all other areas of life, we are able to come to the table and collaborate. That is how the human race has come to advance as far as it has. We sit at the conference room table and share medical and technological theories, findings and advancements, so that ideas and products and cures for diseases can keep improving and building upon themselves. That is called innovation.

In their book *The 50th Law*, Robert Greene and Curtis Jackson describe this current barbaric way of thinking so perfectly using the example of Leonardo da Vinci. Da Vinci was a pinnacle of light in the Renaissance, which was an absolute explosion of knowledge. In pre-Renaissance times, however, knowledge was viewed in retrospect as "prejudice and rigid categories of thinking." Da Vinci, on the other hand, was "one of the most original minds in the history of mankind." He studied everything from art to architecture, engineering, weaponry, mechanics, motion, birds and aerodynamics, anatomy, human emotion, and more. The authors further explain,

> His mind would recognize no boundaries; he sought the connections between all natural phenomena.... Many could not understand him. Today we have regressed to a point that resembles the pre-Renaissance. Knowledge has once again hardened into rigid categories, with intellectuals shut off in various ghettos. Intelligent people are considered serious by virtue of how deeply they immerse themselves in one field of study, their viewpoint becoming more

and more myopic.... We end up strangling ourselves in the narrowness of our interests.... Life does not have these conventions; they are mere conventions that we mindlessly abide by.... Da Vinci remains the icon and the inspiration for a new form of knowledge. In this form, what matters are the connections between things, not what separates them.... All of the greatest innovations in history come from an openness to discovery, one leading to another.

I will add that when it comes to the existence of God, we refuse with all of our might to collaborate and mesh our ideas together. We remain barbaric in this one area of life—what we believe about God. Let's evolve. We were not created from nothing.

Part of our evolution requires taking another look at organized religion. I will say more than once in this book that many organized religions are doing absolutely wonderful things in our communities worldwide, and that celebrating and praising God with our fellow man is necessary. But often we carry our religions to a point that we allow ourselves to harbor disdain for our fellow man who may worship God slightly different from the way we do. But as we observe the birds flying in the sky in their perfect formations, they do so in unity. From a distance we perceive no various logos attached to them. Within their species, we do not observe them attacking or killing each other over any various trademarks. I ask you, how are we any different? I know much criticism may target this paragraph as many would argue that we are not animals. But a true belief in God our Creator involves the understanding that He created everything in the entire universe. It is not possible that where we come from has various labels like Coke or Pepsi, Judaism, Christianity, and so on. Nor has such segregation ever been reported from the afterlife.

Many atheists, at least the ones I have come across in my lifetime, can be loving and passionate people. They love their children with all of their hearts and are kind to their fellow man. They are not perfect, as none of us are. Many of them act out in loving and godly ways. The primary frustration that most of them have is that others in the world label themselves according to a religion, live ungodly lives, judge others, adhere to an "us-versus-them" mentality, or even worse, go to war and kill each other over the belief that one brand of religion is better than another. Many atheists are angry. They refuse to believe that religion is a good thing because of the hatred it can cause, and so they refuse to believe in the loving God who created them. However, they have the love of God inside of them whether they like it or not, whether they admit it or not. Later in the book I will review how most religions hold love as the core tenet, yet many of us are blind to this core value because we cannot see past our labels. Again I say, let us evolve. Erase the labels and live out what we claim to believe.

> *These discoveries [of the near-death experience] are generally not what would have been expected from preexisting societal beliefs, religious teachings, or any other source of earthly knowledge.*
> — Dr. Jeffrey Long, *Evidence of the Afterlife*

So, that is basic faith. That is your answer to the first part of the A.B. Principle, Always Believe.

Faith

Hopefully, you are now reaching a common sense belief in your God, your Creator. So let me keep bringing you higher and higher as you read on. Each part of this book is meant to be like a staircase, where each step brings you closer to your ultimate goal of living out your life the way it was meant to be lived, to live as though heaven is here on earth. Let us now navigate the next part of belief, which is "How do I have faith?" or "How do I obtain it?" Simply deciding to "just have faith" is not enough. Let us learn practical ways in which we can live every moment in faith, noticing God's grand plan in every little thing.

Faith is difficult because life is unfair, it is unjust, it is imperfect, things go wrong, tragedies happen, we suffer loss, we make grave mistakes, and we go through heartbreaking times. Faith is complicated. We ask questions, like, "Why?" We ask "When? How?" For many of us who have achieved a basic belief in God and an understanding that the death experience is peaceful, loving, and filled with utter joy, we are left with the confusion of why we have a loving God and yet such a cruel, hateful, and tragic world. The only way I can explain it is that we need to view our lives in reverse. We are not physical creatures forever. Our true selves and our true home are beyond this life in a place of peace. We cannot help but see this world as the place where we will remain for what seems like an eternity, when in fact our time here is over in the blink of an eye. The Bible says that we must keep our minds on things that are eternal. When we start to think of ourselves as spiritual beings having a human experience, then we begin to understand that this is not our home and it is not God's either. When we begin to think this way, we do not get ourselves so caught up in the tribulations of this life. It is not to say that we were not put here to have joy; we were. But keeping in mind that we will be gone shortly can actually help you to enjoy life more—to enjoy your children, your families, the sunshine, and all of the things that we take for granted when we put all of our stock into this life. So you see, a sad mentality is not necessary to think about death but actually works to your advantage when you revel in life's simple pleasures, knowing they soon will be gone. Placing grand importance on materialism and worldly things is like running on a treadmill, tiring yourself out, and yet getting nowhere of any significance. Of course, we all have the awareness of death, but it should change the way you look at your life.

There have been so many times when my children were running around the house, being typical, rowdy children, making messes, and creating much noise, but most important they were laughing and giggling. In my early years of motherhood, I would have screamed and yelled to stop the noise and the messes. Now, however, while I certainly teach my children the lessons of cleaning up after oneself, I find myself leaning on the wall at the doorway to my family room, just watching, observing as they run around like wild monkeys, with a bittersweet smile, knowing that I will never again experience that particular moment. So I soak it up into my mental pictures and lock it away in my heart. I realize that much of these types of revelations come naturally with age and experience. My goal, however, is to educate the young and inexperienced so that they can live in this joy early, before it is too late, before these moments are lost to frustration, before they have lost everything and only then truly appreciate what they once had.

There is such a joy and peace when you finally realize that you are a spiritual being. I am reminded of the character Neo in the final scene of *The Matrix*, when he is standing on a busy city street corner looking at all of the hustling and bustling of the crowds around him. The look on his face is one of a reassured comfort and peace, a knowing that he is not of this world, and he flies into the air with no doubts or fears. That is the kind of fearless confidence and faith I am talking about. We are not of this world; this is not our eternity.

> *You don't have to understand. You just have to believe.*
> — From Tinker Bell and the Great Fairy Rescue

When you are going through things and being tested, it really is easier to just give up than struggle through. It is harder to endure, to persevere. The very tribulations and trials that you go through are meant to strengthen your faith. God will bring you down to the eleventh hour over and over until you finally get it. With each and every trial, we have the ability to apply our Sound Thought Principle and fight off complaining, worry, and fear. It is a training of our minds and will. It is our "school." There *is* a reason for everything. We may not understand, but we do not have to understand. Many people who have died and experienced an afterlife before being resuscitated report that they now have an understanding that good and bad things all happen for a purpose. Someday, we *will* understand.

> *I know what it is to be in need, and I know what it is to have plenty. I have learned the secret of being content in any and every situation, whether well fed or hungry, whether living in plenty or in want.*
> — Phil. 4:12 (NIV)

Even if your outcome in a certain situation is not, by earthly standards, favorable, you *can* be happy in all things. We can feel happy, honored, and even amazed when we come to realize that we are part of a heavenly and universal plan. There have been countless times in my life when I worried, cried, and prayed as I came down to the crux of a crisis of some sort—*countless* times. But I always asked for God's help. Sure enough, at the very last second, God repeatedly came through and my needs were met. I always had what I needed. This happened so many times that eventually I learned of an ideal way to pray. I became increasingly open and honest with God. I began to tell God, very frankly, that I felt uncomfortable but that I knew He was working on my behalf and I trusted Him. Being uncomfortable did not mean that I did not trust God. I just told Him exactly how I was feeling. This happened so many times that I began to realize that any discomfort or uneasiness that I professed to God would in retrospect make me feel foolish when my need was met. Finally, after years of the same pattern of me worrying and God providing, and when a new crisis or situation came about, I felt the confidence, the astounding, unwavering, undoubting faith that I now have today, even if my outcome was at times unfavorable. Looking back I know that things do not work out according to my plan but God's plan. In retrospect, I would initially be disappointed that things did not work out my way, but now I know they would not have been the best for me anyway and that God had something different in mind. Or I looked back and found that an unfortunate situation taught me lessons that allowed me to help someone else. Often I was absolutely certain that a solution to a problem had presented itself. I was sure. That was *it*. But strangely enough, more times than I can count, I was redirected to an answer I had never expected. Eventually, I actually faced a challenge feeling a bit of peace and even excitement because I could not wait to see what God would do, as He always resolved the situation so much better than I could have on my own. Over time, I decided to replace fear and worry with this excitement. I learned what it meant to truly have unwavering faith. But it took time and countless lessons to get there. There was *always* an obvious reason that would eventually reveal itself of why things happened a certain way, but it never did so while I was in the middle of the challenge.

You must be seeking God and His ways to even begin to understand. You must seek a deeper meaning and divine plan in every circumstance. If you do not, it is so easy to simply see the very surface of a situation, and get angry or frustrated when things do not go according to your own plan. You must let go and let God be God. My motto is "God will zig when I think He is going to zag." I stopped my own planning. I stopped trying to figure everything out, and I fully surrendered. I gave God the control of my life, and it is beautiful. Now I just say to Him, "God, I am not sure what you are doing this time, but I trust you." You can too. It can be quite an exciting adventure when you approach your life in this way. When you ask Him, He will never leave your side.

Life is either a daring adventure or nothing.
— Helen Keller

I have looked at all of my children when they were babies, and as they grew into innocent little toddlers, the same way I think God is looking at me, or all of us, at times. My babies did not understand all that I was doing for them and their care. They lived in the moment and truly could not grasp the love I have for them. They did not see what went on "behind the scenes" and still don't even now that they are older. If I left them in a playpen momentarily to grab a toy or a clean diaper, they cried out as they felt abandoned and feared I would not return. If I took a small, sharp object from a pair of little hands, my child would scream as though I was trying to remove all enjoyment. If I placed them in their cribs in a dark and quiet room because I knew that rest was much needed, they lashed out from loneliness and fear. If I removed a bottle from their line of vision to warm it up, they would scream and cry as if I intended to starve them. Yet in the end, they always ended up dry, rested, fed, and safe, and I saw their smiles once again. I laugh to myself; if they had only known what I was doing in that time that they were crying, they would not have cried at all. They would have had faith and complete trust in my love for them. They would know that safety and comfort were on the way. They would have felt elation and joy knowing that something wonderful was in the works in the time that they were waiting. And so it is with life. God is always working on His will for our lives. He is doing what is best, even if it is a painful lesson learned or something we can turn around and use to help another. Even if we do realize or see what God is trying to do with our lives, there are things going on that we will never fully understand while we are in these bodies in this temporary home. Many times, He will keep us warm and dry and safe, and many times we will be left feeling uncomfortable, not understanding. But God is God. His ways are not our ways. If we have an eternal home in heaven, then we need to trust that the goals of heaven are more important than the world's. No matter how much we expect goodness, rewards, and even perfection from God, the truth is that we will not live forever. Tragedies will happen, and we will suffer the loss of loved ones. What matters is what we do with these situations. Do we use them as opportunities to love or help another? Or do we let them drag us into misery for a lifetime? There is so much beauty, so many wonderful gifts in this life, but on the other side of this life is where we will find perfection.

> *For our light and momentary troubles are achieving*
> *for us an eternal glory that far outweighs them all.*
> — 2 Cor. 4:17 (NIV)

We ask why, when, and how. The answers are coming. They may not arrive until we leave this earth, but many may come while we are still here. The fact is that the answers *are* coming. Sooner or later, we *will* understand. Life will teach us lessons that we will be glad we learned. Yes, faith is hard. Applying the Sound Thought Principle to your faith, will you believe the thoughts that cause worry, doubt, and fear? Or will you believe the thoughts that say, "I don't understand this and I may be uncomfortable, but God has a plan for me"?

In God's realm, life has a very different meaning than it does to us. The meaning of life can be summed up in one phrase—we are here to love and to help others. We were *not* put on this earth to consume and consume until we suck the planet dry. We are here to love one another and to help our fellow man—period. Plain and simple. Billions of times, man has pondered the questions "Why are we here?" and "What is it all for?" I will make a bold and courageous move here and show the answer to these timeless questions. The meaning of life can be summed up in 2 Corinthians 1: 3–4 (NLT), which says, "God is our merciful Father and the source of all comfort. He comforts us in all our troubles so that we can comfort others. When they are troubled, we will be able to give them the same comfort that God has given us."

We need to be more mindful of finding a purpose for our pain. This means we have two choices when we go through trouble and challenges. We can either let them destroy us, devastate us, and cause us to drown in a sea of self-pity and sorrow, or we can recognize that God is giving us lessons to learn so that we can be an example to someone, give back to our newfound cause, or help someone else to avoid making our mistakes. Romans 8:28 (NLT) says, "And we know that God causes everything to work together for the good of those who love God and are called according to His purpose for them." This is an important part of faith because we can come to know and understand that the plan for our lives is far above and beyond what we can comprehend. We can feel a sense of great contribution to mankind when we utilize our unique set of experiences and gifts to better the small piece that we each have been given that ultimately fits into a great blueprint. If we suffer, we can know that it is *not* for nothing at all.

Faith: Real and Powerful Prayer

You have to speak to God about everything. Prayer is so important. The Bible says in James 4:2 (NLT), "Yet you don't have what you want because you don't ask God for it." I ask God for everything. I talk to Him about everything. It is time that prayer not be seen as something you have to do on your knees, repeating phrases over and over again. Prayer for me used to be a one-way conversation in which I would blurt out my concerns into thin air, not thinking about where my words went, only to continue my day in more worry and frustration. Prayer needs to evolve and to fit the practical needs and lifestyles of these modern times. I speak to God all day every day, in my car, in the shower, at my kitchen sink. I talk to Him about everything that I need and everyone I am concerned about. I speak to Him openly, honestly, boldly, and specifically. I pray about anything from a need for fifty-eight dollars to a specific need to gain wisdom in finding a remedy for a painful skin condition. I cannot tell you how many times that God has come through. The time I needed fifty-eight dollars, I received a check from a friend for fifty-eight dollars to repay a favor I had done for her a long time before and had forgotten about. One week, I had no money to even buy another tube of my favorite lip gloss that had run out. Out of the blue, someone asked me if I wanted the lip gloss that she had purchased and did not care for, and it was the exact one that I wanted. As a single mother, raising my kids on my own, I was having a very difficult time financially and often feared the worst. I once pulled my car over to the side of the road because I was crying and needed to pray for a good job opportunity. After crying to God and wiping away my tears, I looked down at the road and saw that someone had spray painted the word *Job* on the curb. I never could explain why someone would do that, but in a strange way, it offered me comfort. That week, I was called in for an interview and got an amazing job that helped me to raise my children for the next few years. I even had people dropping off bags of toys and clothes for my children at my doorstep when I prayed for help with affording clothes! After this happened countless times in the little things and in the more significant things, I realized that this was a two-way conversation, and the pattern continues today more than ever.

I slowly began to realize just how amazing a relationship with God really is. Requests and needs turned into tears of joy and thankfulness. My conversations with God kept reaching new heights, where at times I told Him how amazing I think He is. But I never would have seen the beauty of this relationship if I did not call on Him at all times. You cannot talk to a friend on the phone unless you pick up the phone and dial her number. If you do not make the call, then what gives you the right to wonder why she is not speaking to you? So many times, I prayed for something and forgot about it, and then days, weeks, months, or even years later, I would come across an article, hear something on the radio, or see something happen that would so specifically answer my prayer or even just comfort me in some way. There have even been times when I was just wishing for something small, and a friend or relative would provide it for me, without my even needing to say a word. Over time and through this process, my faith built up to an unimaginable level. God is so amazing. You will never know or understand unless you try to talk to Him. It is a process that builds momentum very slowly. When you begin to speak to God regularly, you will find that, suddenly, things that you hear, read, or experience will become "illuminated." In other words, when you are asking questions of God, what you then "hear" in return will hold a more significant meaning or jump out at you like never before.

At a very sad time in my life, I walked around with a note written to God in my purse. That note asked God to simply "save my life" as I was at the lowest and most devastating point of my existence. Not only did He save my life but also taught me things and provided for me in ways that were nothing short of miraculous. I just dare you to make it a daily habit, even if you feel silly at first, and watch what happens in your life. Remember that it can hurt for a while as God may need to teach you painful lessons before even thinking about answering a request. Other prayers may be instantly answered.

I believe a day will come when praying and talking to our Creator will be popular and mainstream, not something prohibited in all facets of life for the fear of offending someone. We cannot simply go to our place of worship once a week, recite prayers and chants that we know by heart, come home, and *not* acknowledge God in everything we do and still expect things to work out in our lives. That is *not* knowing God. Many of us feel uncomfortable praying. If that is the case, just talk to Him as you would a friend. The Bible says to pray without ceasing. If my children approached me only once a week and sang "Mary Had a Little Lamb" to me but did not speak to me for the remainder of the week, never expressed their needs or thanked me, and then went around complaining about their lives even though I was waiting in the wings ready to nurture and help them, I would be utterly devastated. It is the same with God. What is so uncool about knowing and talking to the being that created us? That is so incredible! If someone told you that you could have a relationship with the Creator of the entire universe, wouldn't you say "Wow! Really? That is so amazing!" You can! You just have to start.

The Bible says (Is. 65:24 NLT) , "I will answer them before they even call to me." God knows what you are thinking and what is in your heart anyway. If you are hurting or you have a need, why wouldn't you reach out for the help and comfort that is available to you? Again, I implore you to just try it. Test it if you do not believe me. If you seek God, you will find Him. He is always working. There are things that you do not see that are happening and being organized and prepared for you that could take years to come to fruition. Do not give up. God may need for you to go through some things, teach you life lessons, and even make you a better person before He is ready to answer your prayer. How sad it is when the runner collapses just before the finish line. It is too easy to ask God for something and, when it does not happen in two weeks, give up or even get angry with God. That is not faith. Pray, pray, pray. Pray always and everywhere. Talk to God wherever you are, on the go if you must. He is listening. God wants to transform us into loving and compassionate people. Remember that when you pray, may it not be for greed but for provision, strength, and the sake of others. Prayer, too, is an opportunity to love and help our fellow man. When your heart is sincere, provision naturally comes to you. Prayer is so powerful, and through it we can change the world.

In the fields of psychology and psychiatry, it is well documented that individuals who possess a strong and unwavering faith live longer and healthier lives. Medical journals and other texts have published articles saying that evidence shows that faith and prayer improve recovery from illnesses and provide powerful benefits to overall health. Those who pray regularly suffer less from depression. Again, this is more evidence of how having a relationship with God is the way we were engineered to live. It all goes back to the premise discussed earlier in this book of how believing, not doubting, is a form of positive thought and contributes to our overall health. This is another way we can turn the

World Health Organization's predictions of depression leading to the global burden of disease on their heads.

> *The highest and noblest use you can make of your mind is by development of a sixth sense through which you may communicate with the Source of all Wisdom when you pray. And the more you depend upon prayer for guidance in all of your acts, the stronger will your mind power become, until there will come a time when you may communicate with Infinite Intelligence instantaneously at will. The late Charles P. Steinmetz once expressed the belief that the time would come when the act of prayer would be as scientific and as definite as the rules of mathematics or the laws of physics. Other great thinkers have expressed a similar belief.*
>
> — Napoleon Hill

I believe that there will be a time when prayer and communication with God will be as mainstream as driving a car or owning a cell phone. I believe that time is now.

Faith and Fear

> *What happened to the grand dreams of our youth? Suicide. Struck down by our own caution, our own lack of faith in ourselves and our abilities. Opportunities? There were many. But always there was risk. Do we dare? We vacillate. Time hurries*

> *by. We anguish…. Finally, we convince ourselves that it's too late and settle for cheap imitations of life. We envy the achievers. How lucky they are.*
> — Og Mandino, from *The Choice*

Fear is the biggest obstacle to accomplishing anything at all in this life. We are our own worst enemies, and we sabotage everything we do. You have to buckle up and hold on tight because life is a rough ride. I have said so many times that we are a stubborn human race. We *can* hold on tight. We *can* use our stubbornness to refuse to give up and believe the promises of God. It is better to take action and to fail than to do nothing at all!

I spent several years literally staring out a window in depression because I had a vision in my mind of putting this book together but was completely paralyzed by the fear and worry of how it would all play out. So I did nothing. I did enough to function and care for my family, but other than that I was frozen. I imagined that I was a lone swimmer in the giant ocean and all I had was myself and my small paddling feet to turn the giant cruise ship around. That is how impossible the task felt to me. Every day was a prayer for strength and determination. I felt as if I was crawling my way out of a pit with my limbs falling off. But I made it through. It felt like a war to me, but there was no way I was giving into fear. And now I sit typing feverishly and as fast as lightning. Now I am so enthused as I have completely conquered everything that was holding me back. My faith paid off. It was worth the wait and all of the painful lessons that it took me to get here. It took me *years* to do it. You can too. Psalm 118:5-6 (NLT) says, "The Lord answered me and set me free. The Lord is for me so I will have no fear." No fear!

> *Do not fear, for I am with you. Do not be dismayed, for I am your God.* —Is. 41:10 (NIV)

Allow me to always go back to the near-death experience. Death is a destination that we must be prepared for in every way. The brave souls who nearly lost their lives completely have gone through their experience for a reason—to communicate to us what we must accomplish in this life. They have commonly expressed that they wasted time in fear and suffering and realize that they are here on earth for a purpose and must complete it. One case study described in *Evidence of the Afterlife* said, "Because of my experience, I am now sharing with everyone I know that miracles are possible in your life every day. After what I have seen, I realize that absolutely anything is possible."

The Universality of Faith: Faith as One World

The concept of faith really is becoming increasingly mainstream. When I use the word *mainstream*, I mean that glimpses of it are everywhere. We just do not realize it. Just like with the Sound Thought Principle, I see themes of faith wherever I go. The phrases "Never give up," "Just believe," "Believe in yourself," and Nike's motto "Just do it" are just a few of the catchphrases that you hear frequently. Secular motivational speakers like Tony Robbins pump us up as they remind us of our powers of choice and action, all faith-based words that drive us and lift our spirits. My youngest child's morning cartoons on Nickelodeon are entrenched with themes of perseverance and "you can do it" chants and songs, and my older children's elementary school has a character-building and upbeat initiative with encouraging signs plastered all over the school walls as they are taught to persevere. The Bible says in Hebrews 10:35–36 (NLT), "Do not throw away this confident trust in the Lord. Remember the great reward it brings you. Patient endurance is what you need now so that you will continue to do God's will. Then you will receive all that he has promised." These are simply a sampling of faith-based influences all around us.

So how is it, I ask, that the world embraces motivational and belief-related themes in the media, from motivational speakers, from music world icons, from our schools, and in spiritual literature, and yet we are still a segregated world? Aren't we all looking for or making the same statements? Why is the message of Jesus Christ thrown out of our government and schools and daily life? Was the Bible's message of unwavering faith really so bad that we aren't encouraged by our political leaders to know about it? Why can Tony Robbins talk about it while Jesus Christ and the Bible are thrown out of the mix? Jesus would have agreed with these positive messages in our modern cultures whether they were given by a rapper, a cartoon character, or a Muslim spiritual teacher. He was all things to all people. Whether we admit it or not, we may have removed the label of "God," but we have not removed His character or teachings. We have taken full credit, and it is not fair.

Such theft of intellectual property would never fly in this litigious world. Let us all get on the same page and come together in our efforts toward one goal, in one philosophy, and as one world. We are doing it anyway, but we slap different labels on our messages as another way that we can remain compartmentalized. We are all saying the same thing. What is so taboo about all of us believing in the Creator of the universe and believing that He can help all of us in all things, no matter what we choose to call Him? Why wouldn't everyone run to the Source that is available to each and every one of us? God is our heavenly father, and He cannot wait for us to acknowledge His presence.

As things go wrong in our lives, let us understand why Jesus, who taught us of God's character, is a practical example to be followed as one who suffered but endured anyway, not a cure-all magic wand that casts a spell over our lives so that we suddenly and magically have faith. When we do not follow His example of strength and courage, we falter, come up short, give up, and do not see things through to the end because we view them as "too hard." Of course, I believe that God can supernaturally help us in our lives. The miracles and healing I have experienced in my own life I would not have obtained on my own without God's help. But the following verse really explains how we can use Jesus's life and death to strengthen our faith, to endure, to take our own race and purpose in life through to the very end and completion, even when the world comes against us and when we struggle through hard times.

Therefore since we are surrounded by such a huge crowd of witnesses to the life of faith, let us strip off every weight that slows us down. Let us run with endurance the race that God has set before us. We do this by keeping our eyes on Jesus, the champion, who initiates and perfects our faith. Because of the joy awaiting him, he endured the cross, disregarding its shame. Think of all the hostility He endured from sinful people, and you won't become weary and give up. Have you forgotten the encouraging words God spoke to you as children? Don't give up when He corrects you. The Lord disciplines those He loves and He punishes each one of us he accepts as His child. God's discipline is always good for us, so that we might share in His holiness. No discipline is enjoyable while it is happening. It is painful. But afterward there will be a peaceful harvest of right living for those who are trained in this way. Take a new grip on your tired hands and strengthen your weak knees. Mark out a straight path for your feet so that those who are weak will not fall but become strong. — From Hebrews 12 (NLT)

Life *is* training, you *are* a warrior, and you *are* becoming stronger and stronger.

Jesus is as practical as any social cognitive psychologist or motivational speaker of our current times. Let us also view our faith as an amazing practical tool in our own daily lives. How do we do it? How do we have faith? How do we believe? Go back to the Sound Thought Principle and apply it to your faith.

But It Hurts ...

For the Spirit God gave us does not make us timid,
but gives us power, love and self-discipline.
— 2 Tim. 1:7 (NIV)

When you ask God for something and are waiting on Him, it can be quite painful. When I was trying to heal in my own life, I knew that something big was happening. I knew that something was on the way. I just did not know exactly what that "something" was. Somehow, though, I knew that God was working in my life and that, sooner or later, I would be used in a big way to help others heal. On the other hand, however, it was the most confusing, devastating, and painful time of my entire life. It seemed as though I was shedding layer after layer of things that were wrong with me—anger, selfishness, financial issues, relationships, attitudes, and unforgiveness—when all I wanted to do was skip all of that and get to the final result. I had to learn countless lessons before I could get to where I needed to be, where I felt God really wanted me, which is right here, right now, at this very moment in time as I type these words for you to read. I had to ask God to keep showing me the next lesson, the next step, the next hurdle. I did not ask Him to teleport me to the finish line. It did not and could not happen overnight. Think about the horror of being stuck in a burning building. Rescuers, firefighters, are on their way to save you. They can find you, yes, however please realize that there may be much danger, smoke, and debris that they must carry you through before you reach safety. Waiting on God can feel agonizingly similar.

As I learned more and more about myself and grew emotionally and spiritually, I found God to be more and more amazing as I kept coming up higher and higher. I could have so easily given up or even gotten angry at life and God when I was learning my life lessons. If I had, I would not have reached the goal of writing this book. I never thought I would get this far; the road was very, very long. But I did! I held on tight for the rough ride and argued with my mind for years, and God won!

We must not regret the past. We must not worry about the future. We have no choice but to carry out each day's tasks until they equal a lifetime of accomplishment. I am reminded of the innocent character Andy in the classic movie *The Shawshank Redemption*. What patience, what endurance, and what perseverance he had. With a few spoonfuls of dirt removed from his wall each day for twenty years, he met his goal. He was finally free. We can all do the same. What are the spoonfuls of dirt that you can dig from your wall each and every day to get you to where you need to be? Just allow yourself to grow. Know that God is working. Use each failure as another step to success. Let God work with you on every facet of your life. You are a work in progress, not an end product.

For me, I know that my life journey of learning and accomplishment is far from over and that, after this book is published, I have much more to do. It is not over, and new and amazing discoveries are still to be found in the future. Life is a journey, not a destination, as they say. Be patient. Knowing God takes a lifetime. Come up higher and higher. Ask Him at every step to show you how.

When trouble comes your way, consider it an opportunity for great joy. For you know that when your faith is tested, your endurance has a chance to grow. So let it grow. For when your endurance is fully developed you will be perfect and complete, needing nothing. If you need wisdom, ask your generous God. He will give it to you. But be sure that your faith is in God alone and do not waver.
— James 1:2-6 (NLT)

God blesses those who patiently endure testing and temptation. Afterward they will receive the crown of life that God has promised to those who love Him. — James 1:12 (NLT)

Prayer for the A.B. Principle

Dear God,

Life is long, and I know you have a purpose for me. Make your desires and my desires the same. Strengthen my faith. Give me courage. Give me patience. Please remove doubt and fear from my heart and mind. I know you will never leave me. I am uncomfortable and struggling with things I do not understand. When I do not know what to say to you, then please know my heart. I know one day you will show me the reason for everything I am going through.

As I work to reach my goals, help me with each and every step. If I need to learn some lessons first, show me what I must learn to become a better person and to reach my goals. Show me God. Please surround me with your shield of protection so that I only hear from you. Close my ears to negative thoughts that tempt me to give up. If I am on the wrong path, steer me back to the path you would have me on. Close all of the wrong doors and open all of the right ones. My life is an exciting journey, and I will ask you every day to keep showing me new things. If I can use my experiences, my hurt, and my pain to help others, then show me who I can help. Thank you for showing me the way in which I should go. I will no longer frustrate myself trying to figure everything out and do everything myself. I need your help. I surrender to you and your plan for my life. I trust you completely even if I do not understand. Amen.

Chapter Four

Life of Excellence: The L.E. Principle

Within the STABLE philosophy, one cannot achieve a life of excellence without first having mastered their own Sound Thought and Always Believe Principles. STABLE is a lifelong commitment, a mountain that you must climb slowly, steadily, and purposefully until you reach the gorgeous summit. There may be particularly steep and rocky parts, and you may slip and fall and have to begin part or all of your climb again. Once you reach what you consider to be the top, you will always stumble and have to reach the utmost heights once again. But STABLE is a tool for you to use in your life so that you can live in supreme quality and truly live out God's will for your life. As with life, STABLE is also not a destination but a journey. Practice, practice, practice. First apply Sound Thought to Always Believe and then apply those two concepts to Life of Excellence.

What is a Life of Excellence, really? Well, it encompasses our entire lives as it applies to absolutely everything we do. The excellence in our lives is determined by how we treat others, how we treat animals, how we treat the earth, words that we say, how we handle our relationships, whether we achieve our goals, the habits we develop, the temptations we resist, the choices we make, and so on. As the STABLE way of living is centered on what happens to us and what we experience when we leave this earth, you now know, having read this far into the book, that love is to be our guide in all that we do. Near-death experience cases commonly report that how they treated others during their lives was one of the most profound and vivid recollections presented to them at the time of their deaths. They describe the experience as being more realistic than life on earth. One case study in *Evidence of the Afterlife* described a recollection of her life:

Everything I ever thought, did, said, hated, helped, did not help, should have helped was shown in front of me ... how mean I'd been to people, how I could have helped them, how mean I was to animals! Yes! Even the animals had had feelings. It was horrible.... I saw how my acting, or not acting, rippled in effect towards other people and their lives. It wasn't until then that I understood how each little decision or choice affects the world.... Strangely, ... I felt a compassion.... It was peaceful. My life has [changed] because I take into account more the feelings of others when I act.

This chapter will explore more ways in which we can live as if heaven were on earth, all the while keeping love at the forefront of our minds.

Choosing Our Words

> *Kind words are like honey—sweet to the soul and*
> *healthy for the body.* — Prov. 16:24 (NLT)

Words can wreak havoc on a life, or they can make a life happy and successful. In each and every one of us lies the power to affect or change another's life just by the very choices of words that we make every day. We are formed by the words that are directed to and about us. Our view of ourselves is molded by the input of our parents, siblings, teachers, friends, peers, and spouses. Unkind words come in many forms and can damage one's spirit, especially if heard repeatedly. Humans have a basic need to be treated with respect and dignity and corrected with understanding and compassion.

Words are so very powerful. They are like an invisible weapon that can lead someone to accept a false reality. There are entire books on the subject of words as these invisible wounds can run very deep into one's soul. A child who is told repeatedly that he or she will never amount to anything will either grow up and succumb to those words, utterly giving up, or go through a tremendous number of painful lessons and challenges to invalidate those wretched words. A woman whose spouse tells her that she just cannot do enough no matter how hard she works, mocks her about her aging looks, or threatens with physical harm and violent words will be trapped in a world of disillusionment and confusion, wondering why she simply is not good enough for her spouse and becoming horribly depressed and insecure. The child, the spouse, the target of hurtful words feels unloved. Some will overcome; some will not. It can be tragic. The cycle is often repeated from one generation to the next. Tactless words leave our mouths like a rippling wave that reaches many.

Words are so very powerful. Do we gossip and spread rumors? Do we complain and feel the need to vent constantly? I certainly could dedicate an entire book just to this subject alone. Instead, let me use a simple analogy to show how the words we choose not only affect others but also affect the quality of our own lives. You see, it is a two-way street. We all want to live better lives, so if there must be a selfish motive behind living better, so be it. It's a type of reverse psychology, if you will. If you want a better life, then be aware of the words you are using in all communications. That is the solution—awareness! Like a boomerang, it will come back to you.

Allow me to use this simple metaphor: You are a light. Think of yourself as the light on your porch. Then, think of all the people you associate with as little flying bugs. It is dark outside. When you, the light, come on, what happens? All of the glorious and beautiful little bugs come to you, swarming all around, wanting to be near your warm and glowing light. In contrast, when the light, is off, you are dark. You turn cold. The bugs fly away as they no longer wish to be near you. Now take this a step further and see your light as the words you choose. When you are "on," you are described by others as one who never complains, never says a bad word about anyone, and sees the best in everyone and every circumstance (not that you have never been wronged, of course). Don't we all, in fact, revere and respect people like that? Aren't we just naturally drawn to pleasant people because they are just such a delight to be around? We all have flaws, yes. But I personally look for the good in everyone I meet and everyone I know.

Conversely, if our light is off, we wonder why friends and loved ones no longer want our company. We wonder why we are lonely, why nothing goes right for us. It is because we have turned off our light. We love to complain about everything. We talk and gossip about the flaws we see in everyone, the flaws in every circumstance. We berate our employees, our spouses, and our children. Our words are like a cancer. They are toxic. People leave our lives. We become bitter and angry; we cannot look in the mirror and learn of others' perspectives of us and of how we have treated them. This cycle makes us insecure and filled with hurt, so we attempt to lift ourselves up by putting others down further. We are alone, we struggle through life, and we blame everyone else. We see this as an inescapable cycle, if we even recognize it at all.

Here is a perfect example of how to apply the Sound Thought Principle because, ultimately, our thoughts turn into words. When our light is off, we judge others and react before actually knowing them and understanding what pain they might be going through. The whole world is allegedly seeking direction on the evolution of consciousness. Well, here is a giant cue. We humans can evolve in our minds. We can move up higher, to a level at which we consider others, ponder their very minds and hearts, and act out in empathy before we see everything as a personal attack and put others down to boost our own egos. We have the ability to break the ice, to lay everything on the table, if you will. Rather than gossip to your coworker about a female coworker, who has been acting a bit irritable, by saying, "Who does she think she is? She is a really moody [expletive], isn't she?" thereby enhancing the tension among all of you, you have been given the gift, the opportunity, to dispel everything with love and understanding. To do this, you must ask yourself, "I wonder what *she* might be going through. I wonder if *she* is hurting and that causes her to act the way she does." You can offer her a friendly smile or a seat next to you at lunch. You can ask her about herself and get to know her.

> *Stop pointing your finger and spreading vicious rumors! Feed the hungry, and help those in trouble. Then your light will shine out from the darkness, and the darkness around you will be as bright as noon.* — Is. 58: 9–10 (NLT)

You can go out of your way to stop gossip. You can break the cycle. Oh, my goodness, when will we stop the cycle, the madness? When will *we* be the ones to show "miserable" people an ounce of kindness and caring instead of judging and backstabbing, which certainly only perpetuate this type of situation? Of course, this office scenario is an example of only one of millions of opportunities we have to undo what we are doing. Let me go out on a really big limb here and say that we—the world—must seriously re-think the way we are living. If the global burden of disease is caused by depression, then we must realize how miserable we really are. Do we want to continue in this way? I say *no*!

> *You think the only people who are people are the people who look and think like you. But if you walk the footsteps of a stranger, you'll learn things you never knew you never knew.*
>
> — "Colors of the Wind", from the motion picture Pocahontas

Let me go on to say that a world covered with Band-Aids is not effective, so let us change on purpose. We have the opportunity to ask our neighbor who is not particularly friendly if everything is all right and offer to help him in any way. We have the opportunity to see when our spouses are suffering in depression or substance abuse, to offer them our empathy and understanding, and to help them with their hurt. Miserable and, at times, nasty people are hurting. That is a fact. It is the time when they are lashing out the most that they truly need us to come up higher and get inside of their souls to understand and comfort them, not judge them and abandon them. Showing another who is behaving sullenly or grouchy a shred of concern can do wonders, break down barriers, and even heal wounds.

We may feel like saying, "What is wrong with you? You are a real [blank]! Look at you, you lazy bum!" Even in the most basic of situations in our day-to-day routines, we can add love to what we say. I will use my husband and the garbage dilemma as an example once again. If he forgets to take out the garbage for two weeks in a row and the garbage is piling up in the garage, I can either say, "What is wrong with you? Are you stupid? Don't you do anything around here?" Or I can say with love, "Honey, I know you have been working really hard and I understand that you are tired, but I really need you to take the garbage out." I know that if the tables were turned, I would be quicker to respond to the nicer version. That really is not very difficult, is it? No, it is not. Furthermore, the nicer version will improve *my* day, as it will most likely return to me in kinder words.

I am not saying we should not speak our minds. We must communicate. However, I know that my husband would not be thrilled about taking out the garbage, or even coming home, for that matter, if I consistently berated him about the simplest of issues. Once again, if I want my life, my marriage, and my relationships to be better, I can take the kinder approach in all that I say instead of just exploding like a volcano when people do not do things or act in ways that please me. I can start with me rather than looking to those around me for happiness.

I am really helping myself by doing this. Yes, I want to be kinder to others, but I also want a better life. I am also thinking of myself when I choose loving words. This is where our choice comes in. This is where we can rise above the anger in our hearts and say, "How can I help you?" "I am here for you," or "I understand you are hurting, and I will be patient." It is amazing how words can melt conflict away, even if just temporarily. I can feel so agitated in my mind and my heart, even feel like screaming, when I am frustrated with another. But the physical act of moving my lips to form words can be separated from my angry emotions. I don't have to feel like sympathizing, but I still have the ability to say things that are sympathetic. I am not saying we should be phonies, either. It is about self-control and breaking a vicious cycle. Eventually, if we practice this long enough, our lives and relationships will improve and the effort will become natural over time. People may start acting more kindly to you, and as a result your own bitterness may begin to disappear. It works! It breaks the cycle! Just like Sound Thought, it requires training.

All too many of us give our mouths free rein and therefore say everything we think. We complain, gossip, and constantly discuss every physical ailment, and no one around us can do anything to please us. Our lights are off. That is not control. That is not evolving. Those of us who say every negative thing we think of to others are left wondering why no one wants to be around us and nothing goes right for us. We make ourselves physically sick by allowing our minds and mouths to hold us captive.

> *On the day of your [religious] fasting, you do as you please and exploit all your workers. Your fasting ends in quarreling and strife.... You cannot fast as you do today and expect your voice to be heard on high.* — Is. 58:3–4 (NIV)

Did you ever notice that people in high places, such successful businesspeople, CEOs, and leaders, do not sit around gossiping and complaining for all to hear? Can you imagine if the president came on TV and complained about how tired he was or if the CEO of a successful international company gossiped about his office staff or laughed at what someone was wearing? Do you typically hear the leaders in your office laughing in the lunchroom about another's choice of shoes? Maybe there are exceptions, but I would venture to say that, for the most part, we do not expect this petty behavior or choice of words from our leaders. Successful individuals tend to speak positively because they are thinking positively. They typically motivate us. They see opportunities in failures. They falter and get right back up again. They focus on getting a job done, and do not waste their time in gossip. That is why they are in charge. That is how they have gained success. Why, then, do most of wonder why *we* are not in high positions, why *we* were not promoted to management? Wake up. Turn on your light. Look at your words. The world around you hears you.

Words form the world's perception of us. Our thoughts and words create our own reality. If I tell everyone that I feel like such a loser and cannot do anything right, then most of the people I know would eventually think of me as a loser who cannot do anything right! Words have an extremely profound effect on us. They form us. They can destroy a family, and they can break a spirit. If we have mastered Sound Thought and are fighting against negative thinking with all of our might, we can also display this victory with our words.

The tongue that brings healing is a tree of life.
— Prov. 15:4 (NIRV)

Choosing Kind Words for Your "Enemies"

Do not be overcome by evil, but overcome evil with good. — Rom. 12:21 (NIV)

We all have people in our lives, I suppose, that we deem as a type of enemy. You may be estranged from an ex-spouse or a sibling, or perhaps you felt wronged by someone you thought was a friend. We have all felt wronged in our lives. However, we have to remember that just as when someone who speaks unkindly to us may be hurting, someone who has hurt us with their actions may have also been filled with incredible pain of their own. We label them as our enemies as we distance ourselves from them. However, without excusing their actions, we can forgive. But forgiveness is for another chapter. In the meantime, in our limited communications with these estranged individuals, we can still rise up. We can evolve. We can have the mercy and compassion that God has for us and speak kindly to them. If nothing else, we can do that—for them, but also for ourselves.

I must share one of the greatest bumper stickers that I ever read. It said, "Be kind to your enemies. It confuses the heck out of them." Now, I know it is not in the nature of God to do anything maliciously, including acting kind. But it simply drives the point home that we really can benefit ourselves by being kind and merciful. We can break a cycle. When we say, "Love conquers all," it really is the truth because who can argue with love? How do you fight with someone who is being kind to you? If a bitter and miserable person has just told someone off and that someone says in response, "I am sorry that you are hurting so badly that you have to treat me in this way, and I hope you find healing," before walking away, how can the person react? How can the argument logically continue? It cannot. Sometimes the kind thing to do with someone who is yelling at us is to do absolutely nothing at all. If I attempted to argue with an inanimate object such as a wall or a door, it certainly would not say anything back to me. I would feel really stupid, cool off, and walk away.

Fighting, arguing, complaining, berating, and gossiping are only forms of negative thoughts and depression that can make us physically sick. How we treat others is what matters when we leave this earth. Let us make it matter now. Watch your careers, home life, and relationships improve and blossom. Be a light in a dark world. Live in the highest quality.

> *Do everything without complaining and arguing.*
> — Phil. 2:14 (NLT)

Let us return to the Pope's question I mentioned at the beginning of this book. How can science contribute to peace on earth? Well, here is where much of it comes together. If your light is on, you are controlling your thoughts in all you do, saying the right things, refusing to think or speak badly about anyone, always believing the positive about yourself and others, living in strong faith, and thankful in all things and not complaining. You see the good in everything. You are purifying your mind, and the toxic chemicals that get released from your brain into your body and then make you sick are diminishing. You are discovering a scientific and biological process to peace. It takes practice and time until we evolve into a peaceful planet. I hope you have just come up to a new level.

Planning for the Future

According to sociologists, humans have a fundamental need to plan for the future. We carry our planners, datebooks, agendas, lists, schedules, and calendars in our tablets and smartphones. We make our calls. We book our appointments. We prepare for our vacations. We stock up on groceries before the big snowstorm, shop for the perfect dress for the event that is months away, educate ourselves for our lifelong careers, and study for tests that are two weeks away. We decorate the nursery for the baby that will be arriving in months, and I could continue. And that is all wonderful stuff.

Yes, it is our fundamental human need to plan and have goals. We are all leaving this earth, and while we certainly do not want to be obsessed with death, this is the one area where we do not think about where we are going. We refuse to plan for this beautiful and inevitable destination. Doing so does not require fear and occupying our thoughts with dying. In contrast, it requires considering how we can live the fullest, most beautiful life possible while we are here on earth. Think about where you are going. Use the scientific study of the near-death experience to help you plan. Will it matter if I drove a Mercedes or a used car? Will it matter if I spoke kindly to my family and took the opportunities to love? Did I frustrate myself and complain that my house was not big enough, or did I focus on empathizing with others and showing them an ounce of kindness? Did I yell at the elderly woman in the parking lot for stealing my parking spot for my Cadillac? Or did I give her a smile and gesture for her to go ahead and take it? Did I scowl at others in the grocery store as I judged each one of them in my mind? Or did I see all as individual souls with their own stories and burdens and offer strangers a smile? This is planning. This is successful living.

> *So we fix our eyes not on what is seen, but what is unseen…. What is unseen is eternal.*
> — 2 Cor. 4:18 (NIV)

Positive Psychology: More on How We Treat Others

> *I realized that I had wasted time in suffering, and what I should have been doing was using my freedom to choose true love, not pain, in all that came into my life. — Evidence of the Afterlife*

How can we see homeless people on the street, walk by them, and go on our merry way to Starbucks for our four-dollar coffee? Just outside the storefront, someone's whole world has completely fallen apart, and a soul has been completely devastated or lost and may have completely given up. They are starving and cold, possibly even at the brink of death. If they were our brothers, our mothers, or our friends, we would kneel down, hold their hands, and tell them everything was going to be all right. We would call the authorities, call a charitable organization to assist them, or help them ourselves. But we have turned into a society that is completely desensitized to a hurting world and are swallowed up by our consumption. It is disgraceful, shocking, and unacceptable. We do not want to be bothered or disrupt our routines, as it would interrupt our quest for the perfect oasis we are seeking that the media and the world have falsely promised us.

> *When I pick up a person from the street, hungry, I give him a plate of rice, a piece of bread, I have satisfied. I have removed that hunger. But a person that is shut out, that feels unwanted, unloved, terrified, the person that has been thrown out from society—that poverty is so hurtable and so much.*
> — Mother Teresa

How can science contribute to peace on earth? Let us explore this question from every angle that we possibly can. Psychology as a formal and researched science is quite young in the history of science and medicine. There is, however, a new school of psychology that has recently emerged at the University of Pennsylvania. Founded by Dr. Martin Seligman, it is appropriately termed Positive Psychology. Dr. Seligman possesses the strong belief that the current state of psychology is "not good enough." Psychology as a science—and when I say *science,* I mean that it is based on scientific methods of controlled testing, research, and conclusions—has since its origins been based primarily on what is wrong with us. Of course, there are conditions and disorders of the mind that can and must be medically treated. However, in this cutting-edge form of psychology being touted at UPenn, it is the researchers' interest to study not what is wrong with us but how we, regular people, can truly find happiness. Dr. Seligman has written and published countless peer-reviewed medical journal articles. His work is truly wonderful, and the world needs to heed his instructions and textbook principles. What is most profound and interesting about study after study of his is that there is nothing but consistent results. He has found time and time again that what leads to true happiness, or what he calls *Authentic Happiness,* is qualities such as altruism, volunteering, donating to charities, and helping others. People who give of themselves are the ones who achieve joy. Furthermore, these qualities lead to not only happier lives but also healthier and longer lives. People who have adopted these principles on their own and who have been involved in Dr. Seligman's studies have reported more happiness and exhilaration than people who have won the lottery. Aren't we all looking for tremendous happiness and peace? If your life is not working and you are depressed, why wouldn't you just put this to the test? Why wouldn't you simply step outside of yourself to help another in some way, and just watch your spirits rise, not just in times of tragedies, hurricanes, or disasters, but rather on any typical day? Helping others is the antidepressant we are all looking for.

Now, let me add that Dr. Seligman reports his findings in a very clinical, professional, and secular fashion. There is no acknowledgement of God in his findings. Yet I will take the liberty here and state that this is more credible support and speaks to the commonality of the messages out there. I fear that Positive Psychology, to some, will be just another "us versus them" or "science versus religion" concept, and we will continue on our merry way to remain a segregated world. However, whether we like it or not, Dr. Seligman's findings are no different from the messages that have been given to us from the afterlife or the messages of most religions and this school of psychology is just another fantastic reinforcement to how we all need to be living. This is the kind of life God wants us to live:

> *Is it not to share your food with the hungry and to provide the poor wanderer with shelter-when you see the naked, to clothe them, and not to turn away from your own flesh and blood ? Then your light will break forth like the dawn, and your healing will quickly appear.* — Is. 58:7–8 (NIV)

Just as the school of Positive Psychology has, didn't Jesus tell us to go out into the world and help our fellow man?

Didn't He tell us that if we follow Him and His ways, we will know God and have peace? Isn't the world today applauding this new school of thought but tossing the Bible out of everything? The Bible was one of the best self-help books ever written! So much of the advice in the Bible is quite similar to what Dr. Seligman's work suggests. So you can understand my confusion as to why there is not yet peace in the world when we all seem to be in agreement.

Do we actually want that peace that Jesus was talking about, or is it something we will just continue to write on our holiday greeting cards as a silly cliché for the remainder of our lives filled with depression? What God has been trying to tell us about is not a mystical fable or magic spell; it is real and needs to be applied to our lives in a very serious way. It is my greatest wish that all of the information in this book will lead you to one conclusion—that we should live in the way we were engineered to live. We were not put here on earth to suffer from such debilitating depression. We are just doing it all wrong.

I once heard a radio talk show host say that Britney Spears allegedly stated that she was the "loneliest woman alive." Now, I am not sure if she still feels that way today, but this is a common feeling among some of the world's wealthiest individuals. Some of the most affluent areas in the United States also report some of the highest incidences of depression. Why is that? Because having money has nothing to do with the way we achieve happiness, and yet it is something we tend to regard as the very highest priority in our lives. It provides comfort and ease of mind, yes. Is it something we should all work for so we can survive and enjoy our lives? Absolutely, yes. But when we have plenty of money and are consumed with wanting more and more—when we have plenty of money and cannot help others with it—that is heartbreaking.

When I heard the reported story about Britney Spears, all I could think was how, if she just stepped outside of herself and used all she had been blessed with to help others, she may not have felt so sad and alone. I know that celebrities are only people and are not immune to sadness, but they also possess unbelievable blessings and power to help this hurting world. I heard it said once that the seven wealthiest people in the world have the ability to erase world hunger, but they do not. And that is deplorable.

> *If someone has enough money to live well and sees a brother or sister in need but shows no compassion, how can God's love be in that person?*
> — 1 John 3:17 (NLT)

A very wealthy individual once paid Jay-Z millions of dollars just to perform at his child's birthday party. Wow, what a difference you could make in the lives of so many hurting people with millions of dollars! People are losing their homes, cannot feed their children, are starving or worse. Do we really need a fleet of fifty cars and three homes? Do we need fifteen purses? Do we really need a new toy every week for our children? Do we need the weekly pedicure when we can paint our toenails at home? There are even middle-class folks with huge nest eggs who watch their fortunes grow, refuse to lend a dime, and hold onto every penny. We all have piles of stuff in our attics and garages that the poor and needy can use. To the wealthy, and even the not so wealthy, I say look at all you have been given. I implore you to dedicate your lives to helping those less fortunate. This is not a judgment of character but a plea for compassion, a plea to recognize your God-given gifts and how they can serve an everlasting purpose. Imagine the problems that could be solved. Think of the lives that could be changed. Think of the smiles that could happen.

> *Oh, the joys of those who are kind to the poor! The Lord rescues them when they are in trouble. The Lord protects them and keeps them alive. He gives them prosperity in the land and rescues them from their enemies.* — Ps. 41:1–2 (NLT)

We all have the ability to share. We may not believe that we are able, but each and every one of us possesses the ability to help others in some way. I am certainly not well-to-do by any stretch of the imagination, but there is always food in my pantry and items in my attic or garage that I am no longer using. There are people on your street whom you can help. There was once a time when I knew I wanted to help others but really did not know where to start. In my conversations with God, I just asked Him to send me someone I could help. That request was instantly answered as I met a new friend with a great need, a wonderful woman struggling to raise her three children by herself. When she came to our home, we opened up our pantry and garage to her as there was so much abundance and blessing there for her to have. The lasting impression it left on her and her children was profound, and the joy that it gave us was immeasurable. Even though I was struggling financially myself, it was amazing just how much I had that I really did not need. I pray that you will ask God to send someone to you. Communities are filled with surplus on one end of the street, while on the other end, parents are not sure how to feed their kids. Families and communities can come together, exchange belongings, and invite one another into their homes. Just look around. Need is everywhere.

Imagine no possessions. I wonder if you can. No need for greed or hunger, a brotherhood of Man. Imagine all the people sharing all the world. You may say I'm a dreamer, but I'm not the only one. I hope someday you'll join us and the world will live as one. — John Lennon

Forgiveness

I will forgive those who are unjust toward me, with no thought as to whether they deserve it or not, because I understand the law through which forgiveness of others strengthens my own character and wipes out the effects of my own transgressions in my subconscious mind. —Napoleon Hill

Refusing to forgive others for their transgressions was once described as holding another in a prison cell for all of eternity. I am certain that no man or woman who has ever walked the earth lived a perfect life. Sooner or later, we all manage to hurt another, intentionally or unintentionally. It is amazing, however, that in this world we are so quick to judge and eternally hold another in the confines of unforgiveness. We are amused and entertained when we see celebrities or political figures involved in scandal. We sit at our dinner tables and revel in the transgressions of popular figures, judge them, and boast of how we could never stoop to their levels. We hear of a neighbor whose marriage has fallen apart, and we gloat as we ask, "Can you believe that she … ?" The fact of the matter is that we judge, we alienate, and we condemn those who hurt us. Often, we even banish them to a life of loneliness, a life with a course that is forever changed and will never be the same because we cannot forgive them. They are left to condemn and torture themselves in their own minds and experience a roadblock in the way of all of their pursuits because we cannot forgive them. We, too, the ones who cannot forgive, feel an unrest and uneasiness for the remainder of our own lives as if a piece of us is missing. It is a life sentence for both.

The near-death experience offers us something quite different. Case study after case study of those who have had a glimpse of the great beyond and returned tell the same story of first acknowledgement, or review, of wrongdoings followed by an incredible compassion and love. When we leave this earth, we feel the unconditional acceptance of a loving God. How sad it is that we cannot receive that from our fellow man.

It is all too easy to love people who are kind to you. It is so much harder to forgive those who have hurt you. However, when you have been wronged, here is yet another opportunity to love. This is just another chance in life to think about how the one who hurt you, or the one who hurts others in general, might be suffering on the inside. Practical Bible teacher Joyce Meyer describes it in the best possible way when she says, "Hurting people hurt people."

But you are a God of forgiveness, gracious, and merciful, slow to become angry and rich in unfailing love. — Neh. 9:17 (NLT)

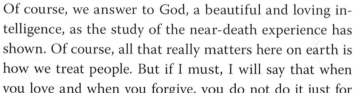

Of course, we answer to God, a beautiful and loving intelligence, as the study of the near-death experience has shown. Of course, all that really matters here on earth is how we treat people. But if I must, I will say that when you love and when you forgive, you do not do it just for others; you also do it for yourself. If you want a Life of Excellence, if you wonder why you have a life of unrest or depression, pain, and sickness, and if you just keep asking yourself when things will ever change, then perhaps there is someone you need to forgive. Do it with yourself in mind first if you must, but just do it!

As forgiveness provides us with countless health advantages, before I continue I must define here how medical professionals and counselors define *forgiveness*. I am sure that this definition is shared by God himself. To truly forgive, one must do good for the offender and even share some sort of transforming journey with that person. It can be challenging, but it can also change your life.

When I was attending graduate school and studying psychology, I came across many articles written by medical professionals with titles such as "Forgiveness Can Improve Cell Function" and "Forgiveness—The Greatest Healer." Such articles described how amazing things happen at the cellular level in our bodies and the great healing benefits of forgiveness. Dr. Caroline Leaf describes in her book *Who Switched Off My Brain?* how the act of genuine forgiveness releases feel-good and healing chemicals into your body. Studies and medical journals reveal that forgiveness has favorable effects on our immune system and even our blood pressure. To harbor unforgiveness, hatred, and bitterness causes much emotional stress on our bodies, which, in turn, reduces the production of "killer cells," or weakens our immune systems, leaving us susceptible to illness and disease. So you see, our bodies were engineered to forgive! We were created in the image of God! Just because medical doctors and psychologists have figured this out does not mean that our compassionate and caring Creator did not design us in this way.

When Jesus said that we are to forgive, He knew what He was talking about. In 1879, a woman by the name of Mary Baker Eddy founded the Church of Jesus Christ, Scientist. Her literary work, entitled *Science and Health with the Key to the Scriptures*, was based on the notion of spiritual healing and healing through prayer. The belief of Christian Science is that healing is directly linked to

Jesus's teachings. There is great truth in this. Scientists and medical professionals now understand the beneficial effects of love and forgiveness on our bodies. Not only do they have the ability to heal, but they also have the ability to prevent forms of illness. Was Jesus Christ a scientist? To some degree, yes. He knew that forgiveness is healthy for our bodies, and that is part of what He was trying to tell us. That is the "peace" He was referring to. He was not simply saying a bunch of warm and fuzzy catchphrases. We cannot wear a cross on a chain around our necks and ignore that there is a scientific and biological formula behind it. It is the truth. It is time to live the correct way.

Forgiveness is contagious. If you want to make a change in the world, then find a hurting person who is hurting you and show him a little bit of mercy. Give to him without expecting anything in return. Speak kindly to him *no matter what*. Simply show him an ounce of kindness. Do you know how much you can heal a hurting soul by doing that? Do you know how that wakes up hurting people? Do you realize how many people have made horrible mistakes in this life and are tormented by guilt and remorse? Do you know how many people are being judged and have been cast out by their own families? Do you know how the simple act of wrapping your arms around a soul who hurt you and saying "It's okay. I forgive you" could forever change a life and bring emotional and physical healing to the transgressor and you, the forgiver?

In my past, I used to love with conditions. I loved people based on how I perceived that they treated me. I internalized everything and kept a mental scorecard when I felt hurt by another's actions and words. In the end, I caused myself much heartache. If I can save one person from doing that, I will have accomplished my goal. The times in my life when I hurt others the most was when I was suffering the most on the inside. Put your arms around your estranged spouse, mother, father, or friend. Say, "You know what? It's okay. I forgive you." Just watch what happens to your mind and your health and your body. Just try it. I know it is so hard. It is hard because we live in a world that does not encourage this practice. We divorce, we sue, and we fight. But who are we to pick and choose which wrongdoings deserve complete banishment and which do not when we too lack the ability to go through life without hurting another? Jesus said, "Let the one who has never sinned throw the first stone!" John 8:7 (NLT).

Let us adopt a new way of living because the road we are going down is bleak. Scientific discoveries related to the human body illustrate that forgiveness is the way. Psychologists state that forgiveness is the way. Jesus said that forgiveness is the way. Religions of the world teach that forgiveness is the way. And when we leave this earth, we will be overwhelmed with unconditional love and forgiveness. So forgive. It is filled with a real and amazing truth that leads to joy and health.

When I think of how much God loves us, I love to use the example of my children, especially when they were babies and toddlers. When they did something wrong or grabbed something that they were not supposed to, I scolded them in a firm and authoritative voice. Upon hearing my displeasure, they instantly looked sad and remorseful and began to cry. Almost always, when they had a sense of sadness over their guilt, they ran to me with their arms stretched up in the air for me to pick them up and hold them. I then held them tightly. I told them that everything was all right and that I loved them. Every time this happened, I felt overwhelmed with love and joy for them, the crying stopped, and I could feel the sense of ease and even joy come over them also. I was no longer thinking about what they had done, only about how my heart ached with love for them. I believe that is how it is with God. We do wrong, yes. But we can run to Him with our arms stretched out, seeking him in our sadness and remorse. If we look for Him and are truly sad for the mistakes we have made, He will once again fill us with joy. He loves us so much, and we are His children.

> *Love your enemies. Do good to those who hate you. Bless those who curse you and pray for those who hurt you.... When things are taken away from you, do not try to get them back.... If you love only those who love you, why should you get any credit for that?... Love your enemies. Do good to them. Lend to them without expecting to be repaid....Then your reward from Heaven will be very great and you will truly be acting as children of the Most High for He is kind to those who are unthankful and wicked. You must be compassionate just as your Father is compassionate.... Forgive others and you will be forgiven.* — Luke 6: 27-37 (NLT)

Handling Conflict and Everyday Problems

Many organized religions of the world teach of peace and that, oftentimes, no reaction is the best reaction. Nonreaction is something people simply cannot argue with. If I screamed and yelled at my car, it would not react. I would feel ridiculous and calm myself down. There was a time in my life when I blew up at every noise, every mess, and everything I perceived to be a flaw or shortcoming in those around me. When people in my life were not living perfectly or treating me perfectly, I lost my temper or even kicked them out of my life for good. Where did that leave me? Lost and alone. I have trained myself to put on a mental seat belt, if you will. When things get chaotic and I feel my nerves flaring, as we have all experienced, I visualize myself holding tightly to what seems to be my safety bar in the sudden drop on the roller coaster of life. This "bracing yourself" practice is necessary because the rough ride is always temporary and the ride always slows down.

When you have lived long enough to realize the ebb and flow of life, the cycles of chaos and quiet, you learn to gently smile through the crazy moments, knowing that the quiet is just around the corner and that the cycle will continue over and over again. I suppose that is why patience tends to come with age. However, what a beautiful world it would be if we were all taught of these high and low tides of patience while we were young and didn't need to learn this valuable lesson the hard way. The hard way involves falling apart at every rough moment, causing irreparable damage to all who are in your path.

I have something I call "tunnel vision." Simply put, when my kitchen is a mess, the kids are arguing, the baby is crying, and the dog is throwing up on the floor, all while I am going through a pile of bills I am not sure how to pay (and yes, this happens quite often), in the natural I could just blow my top. But "tunnel vision" helps me because while all of this is going on, I just briefly look up, out the window, and into the sky. I almost imagine that I am looking through a tunnel, a paper towel roll, or even a telescope. When I do this, I can see nothing around me, only the sky and nothing else. I focus on God for a brief moment, compose myself, and calmly address all that is going on around me, knowing that the quiet is once again moments away. Screaming does not work. It does not work when your kids are arguing, and it does not work when your boss is having a tantrum. It does not work when you are cut off by a bad driver, and it does not work when your spouse is telling you off. Sometimes, no reaction is the best reaction. An irate person will not continue to yell at silence. It is difficult, yes. But practice leads to peace—your own.

Jesus was one who did not react. He took nothing personally and did not internalize anything when he was hurt by others. Here is a man who was mocked, persecuted, beaten, and tortured, yet He knew only how to love unconditionally. He never lashed out. He never fought back. Can you imagine the immense amount of love and peace one would have to be filled with to go through life in such a way? Jesus had tunnel vision; He looked only to God. Jesus said, "My peace be with you"—with *you*! You who are reading this book! You have the ability to remain calm and composed through your troubles. Yes, you. We all have this ability to control our actions because we have a wonderful example of how to handle ourselves through Jesus Christ. There is true meaning in all He has said and done. He was an expert in how to experience true peace. If we utilize His example and live our lives the way He lived His, we will have peace too. When you have peace, you experience the very nature of God. Sound Thought can be used to control your actions here, too. When you choose peaceful thoughts and calm over anger and rage, you do not make your body sick with the toxic chemicals that come from negative thoughts—period. It's plain and simple. It is a very basic, almost mathematical, equation.

> *He was oppressed and he was treated harshly yet he* never said a word. *He was led like a lamb to the slaughter. And as a sheep is silent before the shearers, he did not open his mouth. Unjustly condemned he was led away. No one cared that he died without descendants, that his life was cut short in midstream.... He had done no wrong and had never deceived anyone.... And because of his experience, my righteous servant will make it possible for many to be counted righteous.*
> — Is. 53:7-9, 11 (NLT)

We too can be counted righteous, but we must first adopt a new way of living. Imagine if the whole world adopted this placid and nonconfrontational way of living. Imagine if even political leaders and their constituents were able to rise up in every single situation and, no matter what was done or said to them, proclaim, "No, I want peace. I will be the better person." There is amazing power in that. There are certainly times in life when we need to protect ourselves and our loved ones from danger and extreme or unhealthy situations. There may be times when you simply need to turn and walk away from behavior that is unacceptable. But love and nonreaction are the keys. We have to break the cycle of anger and intolerance in this world. Yelling and strife can ripple out into the world like a wave just as laughter and joy can. Notice the phrase in the above bible verse "he never said a word", calm in the face of death, and yet what a glorious impact Jesus has made on this world. What radical change was brought about by Gandhi's example of peaceful protest. If I react in fury to every hurt or irritation in my life on a daily basis, I will affect everyone around me, and they will spread my toxicity to others. However, if I can be calm and quiet with a smile in the face of adversity, anger has no opportunity to spread and my influence on the world is greater.

You see, even in our daily stresses, we possess the knowledge of the peace that is coming when we all pass from this life to the next. We can react to our problems and every aspect of our lives as though heaven is here on earth. Bills are only papers with numbers. Children will make messes. Dogs will poop on our floors. Coffee cups will spill, and we will have fender benders. To go through our daily stresses without ever saying a harsh word and enduring with patience is the way we were designed to live. Some of the bravest and most courageous people in this world are the ones who can get out of bed day after day with a smile, without complaining, without falling apart, without speaking harshly of another, being kind to their families, and not turning to drugs or alcohol *no matter what each day brings*. When we are young, we look to celebrities and popular figures as our heroes. As we get older, we realize that it is those who can remain humble, quiet, and persistent and do what must always be done without giving up who are the true heroes in life. They are the people in life who are truly blessed. They are the people who are the greatest warriors of all.

I once heard it said that success equals time. Success does not equal the acquisition of money or possessions while we "lose it" on a daily basis. Success means enduring all and remaining STABLE! That is why I love that word and chose it as the acronym on which this entire book would be based. To be stable is the best gift we can give to those around us, to always remain the same in the midst of all storms. When we fall apart, succumb to alcoholism or crime, or act out in violence, we make it clear that we have not learned awareness or gained control of our own minds. When we fall apart, we portray to others that we do not care enough about them to care for ourselves. We spiral downward. We are self-destructive. We falsely lead those around us to wonder why they are not worthy of our love and why they have not provided us with enough happiness as we get drunk, get high, or even commit suicide. To be stable is to rise above our own minds. We are so much more capable of keeping it together than we realize. I am not condemning these types of behavior, as they are worthy of absolute understanding, love, forgiveness, and help. Rather, I am giving encouragement to gain the necessary strength to conquer these horrible demons.

When we can avoid a life of irate behavior and rash deci-sions over a long period of time, there may be bumps in the road, however there is likely to be little tragic loss due to our own mistakes. There was once someone in my life for a very long time about whom I cared and loved very much. Long ago, I gave this person two novelty gifts in recogni-tion of a special and commendable accomplishment. One was an old-fashioned pocket watch. The other was a metal-lic money clip, which I had inscribed with the words "A reminder of your success." I now realize—after strife with and unforgiveness of this person and completely falling apart and therefore losing the person completely—that I should have put that inscription on the pocket watch. The watch represented time and endurance, and how love would have healed all. The amount of money in the money clip now means absolutely nothing.

You see, time is an amazing thing. I have observed married couples go through incredible challenges—alcoholism, infidelity, crushing financial difficulties—who held on and used time as their vehicle to success. Now they enjoy the most beautiful and loving relationships with their spouses because they refused to give up when no one believed they could succeed. They knew that time would heal, and it did. They remained stable, and the storms subsided. In nature there are damaging windstorms and there is blue sky and sunshine. Imagine if we sat through a thunderstorm and proclaimed in our fear, "This storm may ruin my house, so I guess I'll just knock it down myself." That is how we act in life; we sabotage so many things that we do. We neglect to wait for the sun to shine again, but sure enough, it does. And when it does, we are left to pick up the broken pieces because we just could not wait. We just could not hold on.

Look up. Look to God. Talk to Him through all of your stresses. There is a world beyond this one waiting for us. When we get there, let us say that we did not need to have a near-death experience to change the way we lived. Jesus said in John 10:10 (AMP), "I came that they may have and enjoy life, and have it in abundance." His abundance was an abundance of peace. Overreacting, criticizing, cursing, and berating all stem from negative thought processes in our minds that make us physically ill. We can use the Sound Thought and Always Believe Principles in our daily grind, too, choosing patience and endurance and fighting off hostility and defeat. This entire book is one complete process, where one step is mastered and then the next step can be taken.

The way you react when troubles of the world are coming against you really boils down to you and God alone—not you and your spouse, not you and your boss, not you and your next-door neighbor. You and you alone are responsible for your own peace. You and you alone are to satisfy your own soul and lay your head on your pillow each night, knowing that you treated others kindly and kept your calm. It really is not your problem that the world around you is in a constant tantrum. That is their issue with God. Worrying about everyone else's behavior is nothing but a form of control. When you use Jesus as the model of how to live, it does not matter how others treat you. It matters how you treat them. If the whole world would adopt this philosophy, then in the end we would all treat one another wonderfully anyway—goal accomplished. Pray for others. Ask God to bless them and help with whatever may be causing them pain. Be consistent. Be strong. You will not find your angry boss or a grumpy store clerk when you leave this life. You will find God.

Someone once told me that I treat people well who do not deserve it. My response to that was that I treat everyone the same. It is not for me to say if they are worthy or not. I only have one to answer to.

> *In the final analysis, all of this is between you and God.... It was never between you and them anyway.* — Mother Teresa

Control of People and Circumstances

> *Be willing to give an equivalent value for all that you desire.* — Napoleon Hill

If you are able to master the Sound Thought Principle, you are going to feel good about yourself. If you feel good about yourself, you possess "tunnel vision" and let everything else fade into the background, only focusing on treating others well and what God thinks. Then you will naturally be able to let go and allow those around you to freely live their lives. In turn, when you have a healthy mind and self-image, you will naturally live without jealousy, without anger, and without judgment. I once read that mothers who are insecure have more difficulties in getting along with their own children than more secure mothers. I believe this holds true for all of our relationships. When we are comfortable with ourselves, we stop micromanaging everyone around us and become free to grow and blossom in our own lives. When I choose to trust my husband and encourage him to go out and relax with friends on occasion, he is more likely to want to spend more time with me, more so than if I yelled at him every time he needed to go to an infrequent and well-deserved football game. The healthy thoughts in my mind say that he works hard and deserves it. And if I focus more on what I am doing and less on what others are doing, I can pursue my own successes that will help me find my own satisfaction in life.

We need to give up control of others. When we control them and hold them prisoner, eventually they want to escape, defeating the very purpose for which we originally tried to control them in the first place. When we do the opposite—bite our lips, hold our tongues, and give it to God—most of the time our loved ones will flock to us. Let go. Surrender.

Do not sit at home being angry at and brooding over your loved ones because you believe they are not acting the way you want them to and remind them of that every time you are in their presence. That is control and manipulation. We form relationships in our lives with an understanding of how wonderful our spouses, our friends, and our children can make us feel. However, the fact of the matter is that we are not put here on earth to be served by others. We are put here on earth to reach out to and serve others and bring *them* happiness, expecting nothing in return. When you are lonely, call a friend. If you want someone to do something nice for you, do something nice for them. Stop worrying about what the world is doing. Just worry about what you are doing. Get outside of yourself. Naturally, much of it will come back to you, and you will be more fulfilled and satisfied with your relationships. It starts with you.

The energy you spend on complaining that your husband never compliments you can be redirected into finding ways to compliment him. If you do not care for the way you are treated, then treat others better and use kinder words. You see, you cannot control what others are doing. You just have to act on your own initiative. The only control you have at all is over your own actions and words. Change those and then watch the beautiful things that happen in your life.

God's Religion

There seems to be a growing trend the world over regarding religion. Individuals are calling themselves spiritual but not religious, borrowing what they perceive to be the best teachings and qualities of various organized religions, and tailoring them to fit their lifestyles. *Meditation, centering*, and *peace* are all popular terms that we use to calm our chaotic lives. People are tired of the chaos; are tired of religions arguing over who is correct; and see the many organized, institutional religions of the world as the very antithesis of the basic godly cores they were founded upon, even causing hatred and killing. On the other hand, some organized religions are about nothing other than philanthropy. Religions run the gamut from one extreme end of the spectrum to the other, all created and originated with the very best of intentions.

As we look at the near-death experience and the research findings associated with it, we realize, however, that there is only *one* common experience of love from a compassionate intelligence, which is God. God's ways are not the world's ways, and I believe He is asking us to live here on earth the way we will experience heaven—not segregated but working together as one world and for the same goals: love and peace. The Bible states, "Pure and genuine religion in the sight of God the Father means caring for orphans and widows in their distress" James 1:27 (NLT) and "Share your food with the hungry, and give shelter to the homeless. Give clothes to those who need them, and do not hide from relatives who need your help." Isaiah 58:7 (NLT). That is God's religion. Going to a building on Sunday and dismissing a lifestyle of love and giving is *not* God's religion. Living out His religion involves speaking kindly to others, loving unconditionally, accepting ourselves, loving others no matter how different we are from them, and helping others and sharing all we have with them every single day of our lives. That is all. The world is getting smaller and smaller with the Internet and this global economy of ours. We all need to pay attention to the cores of our religions, which are fundamentally the same. We must choose to follow God's ways and not our own. The world must be conscious of its common goals, or we will be forever doomed to conflict.

When Jesus said that the only way to come to God our Father was through Him, he did not intend for us to build lavish churches filled with gold where we could go and feel better than our fellow man, Buddhist, Muslim, or Jew. We are to exemplify Jesus's life. We are to come to our Creator by living a life of love and serving others, just as Jesus and many other benevolent men have done. Jesus did not intend for us to use him as a means for judging others and claiming that we are more righteous. If you believe in Jesus Christ, you believe in who He is and what He is like. He is humble. He loved *all* of his fellow man. He is the author of our faith. He is the author of our peace. God is not concerned about whether we eat fish on Fridays or not. He is not concerned that we wore a pretty outfit on Sunday. He is not concerned with how much money we spend on our child's bar mitzvah. He is not concerned about how long we chanted. Yes, it is wonderful to come together with our friends and loved ones in worship, as God is truly amazing and deserves our celebration and praise. But what is important to God is how many opportunities we take to love our fellow man—period. And that doesn't mean just our fellow man who is the same color, race, and religion as we are, *but all fellow men.* Jesus was all things to all people, and while He walked this earth, He was misunderstood because of this. We reject His ways when we step over the homeless person. We reject His ways when we disregard our hurting brothers who are suffering from alcoholism. We reject His ways when we have money in the bank to spare but cannot offer food or clothing to our neighbors in need. We reject His ways when we will not help or even speak to our Hindu or Muslim neighbors. Those from all religions and all walks of life at the community and international level reject God's ways when we cannot come together in peace and harmony.

> *The greatest among you must be a servant.*
> — Matt. 23:11 (NLT)

> *I tell you the truth, when you refused to help the least of these my brothers and sisters, you were refusing to help me.* — Matt. 25:45 (NLT)

On the other hand, there is so much good going on in the world. There is a growing trend of charitable organizations that are cleaning up the earth, feeding and clothing the poor, helping the sick, helping animals that are suffering, and teaching self-esteem and character to our children. Yet we throw out the word *God* in everything. Like it or not folks, we are becoming more and more godly, all of us. So there you have it. Let us finally admit that we act in benevolence not by our own volition but because we are children of God, and deep down it is in our nature to be like Him.

I will end this brief section with a little story that I found amusing, just something I want you to think about. I once heard a story of a church group (I will not mention affiliation) that had spent much time and energy putting together a public musical mockery of Lady Gaga, one of the world's leading music celebrities, judging her and portraying her as a type of harlot because of her costumes and song lyrics. In contrast, Lady Gaga has dedicated much of her time and efforts to causes like finding a cure for Alzheimer's and AIDS, antibullying, and homelessness because of her deep compassion. She established the Born This Way Foundation, which aims to foster a kinder and more accepting world in which differences and individualities are embraced and that can be safer for today's youth. The list goes on. I end here with this question: Who is acting more in the image of our God—the church group or Lady Gaga?

> *They crush people with unbearable religious demands and never lift a finger to ease the burden.*
> — Matt. 23:4 (NLT)

Prayer for a Life of Excellence

Dear God,

With everything I say and do, let me be concerned with the feelings of others in mind. When people are hurting me, allow me to see your beauty within their souls. Allow me to see why they may be hurting, and use me to heal their wounds in any way I can. Allow me to simplify my life. Show me just what my family needs so that I can use any surplus to take care of a poor soul in need. Open my eyes to the hurting in this world, even if it is right on my street. Thank you for the opportunity to praise you in my religious community but always keep love for all mankind at the forefront of my mind and heart. Bring me someone I can help, dear God. Use this love and forgiveness I now have to heal my own life, and bring to me a newfound peace, health, and happiness. Amen.

Chapter Five

The L.E. Principle: Life of Excellence, Dreams and Visions

Harmony and understanding. Sympathy and trust abounding. No more falsehoods or derisions. Golden living dreams of visions. Mystic crystal revelation, and the mind's true liberation.
— "Age of Aquarius" by the Fifth Dimension

By the time you have mastered your own mind, you have no doubt about the existence of your Creator, you regularly communicate with Him about every part of your life, and you have begun a metamorphosis from the inside out. Even if it is years later, after much focus on and practice in adopting this new way of life, you will most likely find a new peace that results from looking at the world from the perspective of the afterlife and interacting with those around you in a completely different way than you are used to. By the time you master these principles, you should be able to communicate with God anywhere and about everything. You should also be able to listen to your "gut feelings" or your inner knowing, which is God guiding you through your days and through your life.

However, even after mastering all of these principles to some degree or another, you may still feel quite lost. Why is that? The last part of the STABLE road map and the last part of having a Life of Excellence will address that very question. This final portion of the Life of Excellence Principle is called "Dreams and Visions" because it involves fulfilling our very purpose here on earth, God's will for our lives. It answers the timeless question, "Why am I here?" As with every other facet of the STABLE philosophy, this final step cannot be fulfilled until you have spent months or years conquering negativity in all of its forms, you have healthy and peaceful Sound Thought, and your faith is strong and you are Always Believing. You cannot find God's truest plan for your life until you have worked on yourself from the inside out, you are treating others kindly and reaching out to anyone in need who has come into your life and you are living a Life of Excellence in every way discussed earlier. This is most certainly not to say that challenges, negativity, and moments of doubt and conflict will not arise regularly but that you will have reached a level of understanding of STABLE where your life feels, for lack of a better word, healthy. Your life should feel as if it is on the right track.

After understanding and applying the STABLE principles to my life, then and only then did I feel that I was truly ready to move forward with God's plan for me. Many times prior I thought I was ready, but I was not. Every time I thought my time had come, I soon found that I actually had more lessons to learn. I had to improve my relationships and my patience and truly accept myself with all of my flaws and mistakes. I saw the goodness of God over and over again as I went through challenge after challenge. It was like military training designed to strengthen my faith. I had to learn to give more of myself, my unconditional love, my help to others. I am still faced with struggles every day of my life. But, very recently, before I sat down to write this book, I had a beautiful revelation as I walked on my wooded property one gorgeous sunny day. I said to myself for the first time in years, "I am at peace with myself."

The final piece of the puzzle is the fruit, the results of it all. It is all about fulfilling our goals. Isn't that what life is really about? We all have goals and visions, and each and every one of us would like to see them fulfilled. I am not talking about unrealistic or fleeting goals like winning the lottery or owning a professional football team, but realistic, attainable goals that we have contemplated for a very long time. It is frustrating when we struggle to meet our goals or feel we cannot reach them. But understand that life is a perfecting process. We need to get through a lot of "stuff" before we can finish what we need to accomplish. For myself, I imagined that it was like foraging through thousands of miles of dense, dark, and dangerous forest before I finally came out into a beautiful field of flowers. I cannot describe my own journey through this process any other way.

Nothing is handed to us. Granted, there are people in this world who are just so radically blessed with health, beauty, outrageous talents, and undeniable visions at a very young age. Right out of the gate, these people flourish and blossom into what the world deems as the picture of fortune and success. However, many of us in this world tend to struggle, to feel lost, and to find ourselves in situations where we feel we do not belong. Many of us possess a certain uneasiness about where we are in life that we cannot place our finger on. Many of us have ideas, visions, and personal goals that we easily give up on and dismiss, mistakenly believing that they are just silly dreams. This final piece of the puzzle is about getting it right, losing that uneasiness, and finding where we truly belong.

> *Do not copy the behavior and customs of this world, but let God transform you into a new person by changing the way you think. Then you will learn to know God's will for you, which is good and pleasing and perfect.* — Rom. 12:2 (NLT)

Let us begin with childhood. I have always been fascinated by the life stories of successful people throughout history—celebrities, athletes, political leaders, musicians, entrepreneurs, inventors, and the list goes on. Even in my day-to-day conversations with friends and acquaintances, I hear the same theme over and over again. It is always the same formula: every life story that is told starts with dreams and visions in childhood.

Every childhood includes habits and interests related to what that person would ultimately become as an adult. Bruce Springsteen had a guitar in hand at a very young age. Babe Ruth learned and focused on playing baseball at the orphanage in which he grew up. Beyoncé was dancing and singing as a little girl. Stefani Germanotta (Lady Gaga) once told her peers that a time would arrive when they could not go anywhere without hearing one of her songs, and Curtis Jackson (50 Cent) was rapping and rhyming as a kid. Stephanie Kwolek, who invented the material Kevlar, was fascinated with an interesting combination of science and fabrics as a young girl. More personally, when my husband was a child, he would gaze at the small, random tile designs on his bathroom floor that were popular at the time, and in his mind he would envision doors, windows, and buildings among them. As an adult, he has now had more than twenty-five successful years in the construction industry. When I was a little girl, as young as five years old, I wrote stories in school about how people were treating each other and thought about how the universe must have been created by God and how atheism could not be the right way. My favorite toy was my Hardy Boys record player with a microphone; I spent countless hours in front of the mirror with that microphone. Now, I enjoy a successful career as a writer and public speaker, and I still love the microphone. How did I know? How did they all know what was to come?

Who we are supposed to be is instilled in us from birth, and it is a gift from God. All of us must pay attention to what we have been thinking about from as far back as we can remember. I mentioned once before in this book that when I was child, I used to mull over the concept of nothingness. I would question, "What if there was no such thing as anything?" Those thoughts used to terrify me. I was so young, and I did not understand them. But here I am at forty years old, and I am now elaborating on that very subject in this book because I have been consumed by these thoughts all of my life.

Our destiny is engrained in us. It is programmed into us. We are all here to serve others in some way, shape, or form. We are all here to be a part of a large and global community, with each part working perfectly with the next, like a spectacular machine. As children, we subconsciously realize where we are going and start practicing our talents immediately.

> *In His grace, God has given us different gifts for doing certain things well.* — Rom. 12:6 (NLT)

> *Everything has already been decided. It was known long ago what each person would be. So, there is no use arguing with God about your destiny.*
> — Ecc. 6:10 (NLT)

When I talk about dreams and visions, I must incorporate Sound Thought because we need to accept who we are and why we are here. I must also incorporate Always Believe as it requires much strength and perseverance to fulfill the purpose God has for each of us. The only way to reach our destinies is to fight for them. Our minds will attempt to stop us. I almost gave up on my own destiny thousands of times, but because I fought the horrible and even nasty voices in my head, I am where I am today.

Most of us are living this life depressed and physically ill from the depression. I believe that much of that is due to the fact that many of us are living outside of God's will for our lives. It is very important that we all find quiet solitude and time to think about what we know to be true, to think about what is really in our hearts. We call it following our instincts, a gut feeling, a knowing, or a sixth sense. Whatever you may call it, some things just feel right. They just flow. There are other things that we cannot explain, but often we just feel uneasy about something or a certain situation, and we do not know exactly why. We all possess this knowing. However, oftentimes we choose to ignore it, and then we don't know why nothing is working, why we are so very frustrated, and why we do not feel peace. I am not talking about the normal frustrations and challenges that we will encounter on a day-to-day basis but the general sense we get from a larger picture. Even people who have no belief in God often feel something pulling at them or calling them in a certain direction. God is speaking to us, seeking us. However, some of us choose not to listen. Even if we do hear these callings, many certainly do not acknowledge that something greater than ourselves is communicating with us. Even if many individuals heed the call on their lives, they all too often give themselves all the credit.

This is a critical aspect of our lives about which we must pray and talk to our God, our Creator, regularly. Every day must be seen as one step closer to our goals, even if success is actually far in the future. I know that I cannot and would not have written this book and gotten to where I am today if it were not for the infinite power of God. I am not sure why it is not mainstream or more popular for all people to seek help from almighty God, who is everywhere and everything at all times. Who would not want this amazing power in their lives? We shy away from it. Our prayers and our regular daily lives are something separate when they need to be meshed together as one to have any real effect on our outcomes.

When we are setting out to accomplish our goals, we need to keep asking, "What is my purpose? What is my next step? "Show me what to do next!" Step by little baby step, you get there! Day by day, week by week, month by month, and year by year, you get there. If you do not feel that you are where you need to be, then ask, "God, I do not feel right about what is going on in my life. Where am I supposed to be?" And while you will *not* just wake up one day and immediately distinguish what your purpose is, you may simply have a feeling in your heart that you cannot quite articulate. Visions in your mind may be fuzzy and unclear. But if you keep on asking, the path will become clearer and clearer.

I used to treat prayer as a one-way street. I would cry out to God regarding all of my concerns and sadness. Like the sock that gets lost in the laundry, never to be seen again, I am not really sure where my prayers went. Over time, I looked back and saw that God had been speaking to me too. Articles would come my way, people would make an impact on me in a big way, I would hear something on TV, and literal miracles and answers to very specific prayers would just happen, always completely relevant to what I had just been asking. I was consistently surprised and often amazed. God was directing me and constantly validating what was on my heart and what I felt He wanted me to do. Most incredibly, He provided the resources to do everything I thought He wanted me to do. As time went on, I felt more and more sure of where I should be in my life until there was no shred of doubt left in my mind. Again, this process took many years and daily conversations with God.

I was at a point, after I had my first two children, that I felt the first call of God on my life. My children were both toddlers. I was cruising along in my life when, suddenly, I had a sensation that great change was coming. I remember looking out a window and viewing the horizon above the trees on a very cloudy and windy day and feeling an over-whelming sense of change, anxiety, and responsibility. At the same time, I felt lost. I did not know where I belonged, even though I had a lovely home and beautiful children. I felt out of place. At the time, I think I chalked it up to fatigue or stress. Now when I look back, I remember it as a very powerful and overwhelming feeling. There was a great unrest inside of me. Little did I know then what was about to happen, that my whole world would be torn apart and I would hit rock bottom.

Now, before I hit the lowest point in my life, I also had what I would call dreams and visions, or in other words, very strong gut feelings. There was an incredible feeling of excitement inside me, almost as if God had given me a brief glimpse of what would be on the other side of rock bottom. I am not attempting to pump myself up in any way, but I had an idea that someday I was going to be well known in some way—successful and standing on a stage doing something, but I did not have a clear idea of what. The feeling I had was like "Wow!" The desire to propel myself forward in some way was so strong, but it also caused me to have the most overwhelming feeling of unrest. My dreams and visions, however, did not turn out the way I would have ever expected or imagined.

It is imperative here that you understand that I am not talking about silly and unrealistic daydreams that come and go. I am talking about concepts that loom in our minds and hearts, eating at us for a long time and in a big way. Many of us experience similar feelings, and herein lies the problem. We all tackle these strong desires in accordance with the way the initial dream or vision is presented to us in our minds and hearts. When it does not work out exactly the way we think it will in a short period of time, we give up. That's it. We put it to rest. We never think about it again, and we say to ourselves, "Boy, that was a stupid idea." That is absolutely wrong. I believe that from its first inception, that initial big dream you have is so strong because it is meant to drive you. God wants to push you out of your seat and get you moving. He wants you to do something, anything, and move you toward your purpose.

> *It will cost you nothing to dream and everything not to.* — Unknown

Sometimes we have to tackle the same dream or vision from five thousand different angles before we can even begin to get it right. When I first felt pulled in one particular direction in my life, around the age of thirty-five, I began to take acting classes. I had known from childhood that I had a love for the microphone and wanted to stand on a stage in some capacity, so I began to attend auditions for commercials and TV shows and signed up with a talent agency. The only thing I knew was that I wanted to be heard in some grand way. I really thought that I was going to be "it," and to be quite honest, I was very pumped up. My desire to succeed was like no other I had ever had in my life. It was an exciting time for me, albeit brief.

Now here is what then transpired. It (being my goals to act and perform) all came to a screeching halt. I hit a brick wall. Nothing that I did worked. That was the very moment in time when I could have laughed at what a dumb idea I had and grieved over my failures. It was the perfect opportunity to put the dream to rest, go back to a regular life, claim a paycheck, and spend the rest of my life wondering what could have been. But if I had done that, it would have eaten me alive for the remainder of my years. What I realize now at forty, now that I am sitting here and writing this book and now that I am doing public speaking based on this book, is that my initial dream and vision had so much validity to it. I always knew I would stand on a stage and speak or have some level of recognition. It is just that in the beginning, when this metaphorical lightning bolt hit me, I did not understand how it would all actually play out.

I spent quite a long time approaching this vision of mine with many different strategies. I also, and very importantly, had to ask God every day to work with me, to keep closing the wrong doors and opening the right ones as I frantically attempted to open every door that I could for years. It was a frustrating and tiring process. I had to ask God every day for strength and wisdom to figure out what He was trying to show me. Month by month, the path became clearer and clearer. I finally found the right angle. It was like a maze that took me almost six years to get through. Six years! What I was supposed to be doing was writing this book and lecturing, motivating all of you and those who come to watch me speak. It was as if I had opened a million doors with an irritated sense of urgency, and 999,999 of them were wrong. When I finally opened the right door, I felt a peace like no other. The enjoyment I feel writing this book is incredible. It flows from my mind and through my fingertips like magic. I have finally found the purpose that called me years ago. This is how it was all supposed to play out.

> *If you can keep on trying after a dozen failures, the seed of a genius is germinating within your soul.*
> — Napoleon Hill

I ask you to use this story as a model for your own attempts at success. Everyone's story and timetable will be different. "Never give up" is a wonderful catchphrase used in our society, but to me, I needed so much more than that. I needed an instruction manual on just *how* to never give up. But it does hold true. Never give up. Just remember that doing the same thing over and over again despite the fact that it does not work is ill advised. Whatever you attempt and feel driven to do, try it a little differently every time.

You have a knowing in your heart. You have to figure it out. If you do not understand it, ask God for wisdom. He will give it to you. The truth is that when you start asking questions, amazing things start to happen. We must all realize that the results will be God's version, not ours. However, His plan is so much better than ours. What I am doing now is so much more amazing to me than what I thought I would be doing. I get to inspire millions. And I thought I would be acting in a toothpaste commercial!

My point is that we must surrender to God's will. Let God be God. If you had plans to have a healthy cooking show on TV but you end up opening a vegetarian restaurant, so be it! If you had plans to be the next female pop star but you end up with a lifelong career of giving singing lessons to little children, so be it! I can guarantee that when God has His way, you will be at peace. Accept His will and His alone. It is far more beautiful than anything our simple minds can imagine.

> *Morning by morning He awakens me and opens my understanding to His will.* — Is. 50:4 (NLT)

If you want to have a relationship with God, you have to put to rest anything that you think you know. I said earlier that some of the smartest people in the world are those who know that they know absolutely nothing, not those who believe that they have everything figured out. Pure genius is complete surrender and communication with God. I got so frustrated with nothing working in my life that I finally said, "You win, God. Have your way with my life. Show me because I do not know where this is going, and I clearly do not know what I am doing." That is when the road became quite smooth and the fog began to clear. His ways are not our ways. We all need to realize our purpose here on earth. When you finally find clarity, do not doubt. Use your Sound Thought and Always Believe Principles to sprint forward, and do not look back. They will be tools that will help you finish your race.

> *God have mercy on the man who doubts what he's sure of.* — Bruce Springsteen

Of course, we must go to work, provide for our families, pay our mortgages, and live up to our responsibilities, but this does not dismiss the fact that we all occasionally get the sense that a new season in our lives is about to emerge. It does not mean that, while you are tending to your job, you cannot pray daily for a resolution to whatever is tugging at your heartstrings or keeping you awake at night.

I heard a story on the radio from a seventy-year-old man who did not respond to a calling on his life. He told of a time when he was in his twenties and felt a very strong and urgent pull to be a missionary. He felt that he belonged in a foreign country, helping the poor and the sick. However, he did not have that tunnel vision that I mentioned previously. He let everything and everyone around him distract him from his purpose. He did not follow the vision that he held in his heart as people told him it would be unsafe, too risky, and inconvenient and that he would have to sacrifice too much. He listened to the world. He ignored God's call and that nudge he felt in his heart. That man, at seventy years old, stated that he has *never* had a day of peace in his life. He always wondered what could have been and lived his life with regret. If you ignore God's call on your life, it will also consume you and leave you with mountains of regret. There is no greater tragedy.

People will attempt to crush your dreams. They will tell you, "It won't work out," "It's a silly idea," or "Who do you think you are?" When you feel as if you are being pulled in a certain direction, you must ask God that you hear *only* from Him. You must ignore everything that can distract you, and I mean *everything*. I reached a point in my life when I did not want to turn on the TV or tell friends or relatives what I was thinking or doing because I was so sure of where I was going that I did not want any negative input or influence to deter me. I know this is extreme, but I was just very focused. I was incredibly driven to the point that I preferred some isolation to complete my work over any option of failure.

Perhaps some of us are perfectly content with following our own minds and everyone else's opinion. Perhaps you are happy to float randomly in the wind, going wherever it takes you, disregarding your gut feelings, and dismissing them as nothing more than that. Perhaps you want to follow the world and all that you hear around you. That is fine. Many of us live like that and are good and happy citizens. Many of us, however, are lost and frustrated. You may know that you are supposed to be somewhere but you do not know how to get there. Martin Luther King Jr. said, "You don't have to see the whole staircase, just take the first step." That is how you need to approach your goals— step by step by step and so on. Eventually, it amounts to the big picture. Here I am at forty years old and finally communicating my message, hopefully to the entire world. I cannot tell you how relieved I feel. I feel as though everything I have ever done in my life and everything I have ever experienced is all just coming together now that I am writing this book and communicating this philosophy to all of you. I am finally fulfilling God's will for me. I was not supposed to stand on a stage and act. I was supposed to teach STABLE on a stage, and that is all.

Be Prepared: It's Going to Be a Rough Ride

> *Failure meant a stripping away of the inessential. I stopped pretending to myself that I was anything other than what I was and began to direct all of my energy to finishing the only work that mattered to me. Had I really succeeded at anything else, I might have never found the determination to succeed in the one area where I truly belonged. I was set free, because my greatest fear had been realized, and I was still alive, and I had an old typewriter and a big idea. And so rock bottom became a solid foundation on which I rebuilt my life.*
>
> — J. K. Rowling, Harvard
> commencement address, 2008

Living as though heaven is on earth means seeking, hearing, and acting upon the plan of heaven for this world no matter how challenging, daunting, or even sad it appears from this world's standards. There is an agenda that is bigger and more meaningful than our daily comings and goings, a plan of another world that we only catch mere glimpses of.

When you are trying to fulfill God's will for your life, you have to be prepared for many obstacles and be incredibly strong. It takes an immense amount of courage to see your purpose to the finish line, especially when it is years away. The reason is that when you have your first taste of a giant dream and vision and you experience your first "wow" moment, it will most certainly not happen in a short period of time, and the excitement that gets you up and moving will most certainly fizzle. It will transform from elation to serious work that you have to get done. But all too often, that changeover from "Wow" to "Now I've got work to do" is where most of us fall down and give up. We see from A to Z but really want nothing to do with B through Y! In the steps between A and Z, you will have doors close in your face. You will open doors too soon and things will not work out because you are in your own timing and not God's. You will experience depression, doubt, and disbelief. You will go through trials that will challenge your integrity and transform your character. God will keep bringing you up higher and higher when you make a commitment to partner with Him. Even so, every time you go up higher, you may be faced with a new challenge. Always remember, as I did, that God will not bring you far into your journey with Him only to drop you. He is just refining you at every stage of the process. I started writing a book five years before I sat down and wrote this one. Because I was attempting to write it too soon, my mind went blank. I could not finish it, and I spent years after that learning many more lessons and being paralyzed with depression. But in that time, I learned so much, got my life together, and healed from internal wounds. In all of that time, I was provided with all of the knowledge that I needed to finally sit down and write. It could not have happened in my own timing.

We have to do it God's way. He will close the wrong doors, lock them, nail them shut, and cover them with a concrete wall so that you can never open them again. You may stand there in defiance and bang on the locked door only to become devastated that it will not open, when all God wants you to do is turn around, walk away from that door, and let Him lead you to a new one. You need to pray every day that God closes the wrong doors and opens the right ones. You do not know where exactly you will end up, but through it all, there will always be that still, soft voice in your heart—that dream, that vision. Most likely, if that vision for your future is strong, you will experience a constant sense of urgency about it. You have to look at it like getting through a maze. That is life. God's voice will always lead you out.

When you see from A to Z but are working on B through Y, you may have to suffer for a while, maybe a long while. After I was struck by the notion that I would be doing something big, something important, in the future, my original enthusiasm turned into a dull knowing sprinkled with confusion and self-doubt. From the time I first imagined what I should be doing in the future, I guess you could say that my ideas took a back seat and were put on hold. I had to stop and suffer for some time while God improved every aspect of my life. I never forgot about my goals, but I saw miracles happen in my finances, my relationships, my thought processes, my faith, my learning and discovery, and even my health. I had to pray every day that God would peel away all of the layers that needed to be removed or improved. I had to pray that I would be humbled (boy, did that lesson hurt!). I had to pray that He would help me with depression, guilt and shame, forgiveness, a home, financial solutions (God and I are still working on that one), direction, timing, and so on. God led me to solutions, helpful resources, or experiences for every facet of my being until I felt whole and at peace with myself. It was a process that made me feel as if I was not going to finish my goal alone but that I had an amazing trainer who knew exactly what it took to get the job done. I saw a pattern in God's goodness in my life like never before. I learned to love Him like I now know He loves me. Throughout this, though, I questioned, "How could I be so sure of something and feel so strongly about it only to have it come to an abrupt stop, followed by years of intense sadness and doubt?" It was a sequence of thoughts and emotions that would undoubtedly lead one to believe that they might be delusional. In retrospect, I see that it had to happen that way.

Over the years I learned so much, and with much research and thought, I slowly developed the philosophy that is now STABLE. Without those years of introspection, intense thought, prayer, and note taking, STABLE would not exist. And it most definitely would not exist if I had given up, like I wanted to a million times. It could not have happened my way. If it had, I would have been an overnight success as an actress or performer of some sort, living a materialistic life with no real eternal meaning. I would not have felt the absolute peace and happiness that I do today. So as the saying goes, "Be careful what you ask for; you just might get it." You just might get it. But if you do it the right way, God's way, life is beautiful.

In everything, be grateful. Through troubles, heartache, doubt, and challenges, be thankful. This is what molds us, what forms us. We are put here on earth to feel something, to have emotions, to learn from mistakes, and to learn from loss. We are humans, not robots. Learning makes us grow and mature. How else would we know? Growing, maturing, and learning help us accomplish our goals and fulfill our purpose. So yes, be thankful in all things. Nothing worth having comes easily.

I have mentioned before this particular Bible verse, and I repeat my strong belief that it truly encompasses the meaning of life.

> *God is our merciful Father and the source of all comfort. He comforts us in all troubles so that we can comfort others. When they are troubled, we will be able to give them the same comfort that God has given us.* — 2 Cor. 1:3–4 (NLT)

How would we know how to help others if we didn't go through difficulties ourselves? Who would then have the compassion to help the sick if we never experienced illness or disease? Who would help feed the poor if we never experienced loss and hunger? Who would know to help kids with insecurities if they themselves had not been bullied? Who? I would not have written this book to share my experiences with you had I not lost everything and lived through great sadness first. You see, when I was hurting, God sent people into my life to help me, and to those wonderful people I am forever grateful. God's plan was to make an unforgettable impression on me of His mercy and goodness. Not only did I want to shout it out to the world, but I could not wait to help others as I was once helped. God can turn the ugliest, most devastating circumstances into great causes. Do not hold your experiences to yourselves; use them to help others!

I understood that everything good and bad happened for a purpose. — Evidence of the Afterlife

The world has led us to believe in a sense of entitlement in that we are supposed to obtain success, wealth, health, and happiness instantaneously. We strive for instant perfection and figuratively bang our heads against the wall when we cannot reach this optical illusion. That is not the way it works. We ask, "Why is this happening to me?" "Why am I going through this?" and "Why do bad things happen to good people?" We pop pills, reach for drugs or alcohol to numb our grief, and perpetuate this mad cycle because we refuse to seek the true meaning behind it all. You can get through it. You can smash through the brick wall. You can plow through it. You *can* have Sound Thought. You *can* Always Believe. You *can* have a Life of Excellence. You can reach your highest and fullest potential, all while suffering along the way and persevering. God is preparing you! Look at all of the people you can help by sharing your experiences.

When we pass on from this earth and see God, there will be no doubt, no loathing of ourselves, and no frustration. There will be only a love like no other and a true understanding of our purpose and responsibilities that we had while we were in a physical body. Let us live that way now. Use every opportunity you have to love others and help them. Your own unique gifts, talents, and experiences are meant to influence, inspire, or comfort. They are meant to be given back to this world.

The final step of this takes you to the other side of suffering, and you finally realize and fulfill your purpose here. When you do, you will take a glimpse back at your original dream and vision, and you may realize that your success does not exactly match your original precognition from the beginning, although it may be similar. We are not clairvoyants, and we cannot see into the future. We are all blessed, though, with some level of basic intuition. To be honest, I like God's version better, and so will you.

Keep Your Head

> *I will find my way. I can go the distance. I'll be there*
> *someday, if I can be strong. I know every mile will*

be worth my while. I would go most anywhere to feel like I belong.

— "Go the Distance" from the motion picture Hercules

To cross your finish line, you must be an absolute warrior. The more you seek God's will, the more the world, people, and circumstances will come against you. Be strong. There may be times when nothing makes sense to you. You just know that you know. Developing the STABLE philosophy and writing this book once consumed me, and my passion for it now is as strong as ever. It used to keep me up at night and occupy my every thought. I would write notes on tissue paper, napkins, Post-It notes, and scrap paper and put them in a large envelope for months until it was overflowing and finally formed the outline for this book. What I was thinking about day and night and what I was doing made no sense to me. There may be times when you are striving toward your goals, and you may feel like you are going crazy. There will be times when you will want to run back to where you started. You will have started out on your journey, the world will come against you, and all you may want to do is run back to what you know, home base, where you are safe with the familiar. Keep moving forward! Sometimes that is the only option you have. When heaven has a plan for you, God will not allow you to look back. Sometimes God will cut you off from any other options so that you have no choice but to do what you believe is in your heart and what you believe God has been telling you to do. There may be times when God asks you to walk away from things that meant everything to you. There may be times when you have to give up physical comfort. But God will provide everything that you need to complete your purpose. I did not say everything that you "want," but everything you "need."

I recall many times in my journey of writing this book when I sought other ventures and placed my writing aside, notes tucked away in a drawer. Even though I sensed a calling, I was attempting to ignore it. So I would beat around the bush. I set out to get a master's degree, open a yoga studio, and get a job. Sure enough, every attempt would not work out. I would fail time and time again. I believed that this book could be a hobby on the side, not a main focus. But every door was slammed in my face. I even reached a point when I had no money, no gas in my car, and nowhere to go but to sit and write. The inessential was stripped away. I did not even have a computer to type this book, but by the grace of God I actually won this computer at a charity dinner right before I started to write. That is when I gave in and focused on this book alone. That is, unexpectedly, when I experienced the greatest peace and joy. It is a time when I could have fallen into a deeper despair and given up completely. And so I encourage you to not battle with God. You will not win. Surrender and live out your purpose when you find it. Tackle your dreams from one angle. If it does not work, try it another way. If that does not work, tackle it a different way. If that does not work, try it that way. You will get there. The path will become clearer and clearer, and the road will open wide. Accept the challenge as great things are on the way. God will never leave you nor forsake you.

Keep on asking, and you will receive what you ask for. Keep on seeking, and you will find. Keep on knocking, and the door will be opened to you.
— Luke 11:9 (NLT)

Many Callings

My child, go back, for you have much work left to do! — Dr. Jeffrey Long, *Evidence of the Afterlife*

You may have more than one calling on your life. You will not necessarily have just one. One may even lead you to the next. When I was much younger, I had a strong desire to be an interior designer. I possessed an incredible passion for color, textures, art, and architecture. It consumed me, and I was as passionate about it then as I am now about the STABLE philosophy and being an author and speaker. I graduated from college with a Bachelor in Fine Arts and enjoyed a fulfilling career designing homes and commercial spaces for sixteen years. I felt very much at peace during that career. For a very long time, I felt as if that was where I was supposed to be. Looking back, I know now that I learned many lessons during that career as a designer that helped shape who I am today in every way. Inevitably, I reached the end of that season and suddenly felt as though I was being pulled in a completely different direction. It was as though the door to my old life had been completely shut, locked, and bolted, never to be experienced again.

If that is the case for you, you may spend as much time mourning your past as I did. Mourning and grieving over change and loss are necessary and normal processes. But you may be left with no other options but to lunge forward as the past can never be undone, no matter how much we grieve for that old career, marriage, or loved one we have lost. Go with it. Many people are going back to school later in life, following new and different passions than they once practiced. People can recover from loss of a loved one, and accept new loved ones into their lives. People can lose everything they have ever worked for and begin again. It is never too late. At the age of thirty-seven, I found myself with nothing. I was bankrupt and suicidal and had only enough possessions to fill the trunk of my car. Now here I am. By now I guess you know the rest of the story.

There is a philosophy or attitude called "Finish Strong" founded by Dan Green. It utilizes stories of great historical and athletic figures of the past and present to inspire men, women, and children of all ages in sports, business, and even spirituality. I stress to you that God may have multiple plans for you in this life, and Finish Strong describes this very well with this quotation: "The Finish Strong attitude is grounded in the principle that you never 'get there' in life and that you should always keep moving forward. When [John Naber was] asked if winning four Olympic gold medals was the highlight of his life, he replied, 'I hope not. I've still got a lot of living left to do, and I hope that my greatest achievement is still in front of me!'"

There will come a time when you believe everything is finished; that will be the beginning.
— Louis L'Amour

Regardless of your age, it is never too late to begin again. God has another phase for you. Finish the work that he has planned for you, and then find your next calling. Many near-death experience case studies report meeting with a loving intelligence that helped them understand that they had purposes yet to fulfill here on earth. Let us not wait for our deaths. Let us work with God and figure this thing called life out now. Let's get it right in one lifetime!

Focus

We know that God causes everything to work together for good for those who love God and are called according to His purpose.
— Rom. 8:28 (NLT)

When you are working toward your goals and achieving your purpose, you cannot and must not care what people think. If you have a knowing in your heart that serves a righteous purpose, do not let yourself be influenced by the world. It is between you and God. Sometimes you will find, as I once did, that you need to say very little. For me, figuring out exactly what I was supposed to be doing was the loneliest and most frustrating time of my life. I know that for some, life comes very easy. But for those of you who are lost, hurting, and tirelessly searching for direction, just go somewhere quiet and close your eyes. Think. Feel. Ask God. See what comes to your heart and mind. Write it down. Do something. Anything. Take that first step, even if it is the wrong one. God will show you.

> *Your time is limited. So don't waste it living some-one else's life. Don't be trapped by dogma, which is living with the results of other people's thinking. Don't let the noise of others' opinions drown out your own inner voice. And most important, have the courage to follow your heart and intuition. They somehow already know what you truly want to become. Everything else is secondary.*
> — Steve Jobs, Apple founder, 2005 Stanford University commencement speech

Remember that it is not just the world that will distract you, but your own thoughts will sidetrack you. Use the Sound Thought Principle even when it comes to achieving your goals. Sometimes it will feel as though everyone and everything is trying to stop you. Always, always, always pray that you hear *only* from God and that all other voices are silenced. Before I began to write this book and before I fully developed STABLE, my mind said, "Maybe I should do this. Maybe I should do that," and it was the most confusing and baffling time. I thought it would never end. I felt, for a while, that God had put me in a prison and cut off everything from my life, eliminated all other opportunities and possibilities until I had no choice but to sit, study, learn, and put all of this together. You may find yourself in the same situation. God is trying to tell you something.

He is not punishing you. He is asking you to finish what you started. Have courage.

> *Believe in the Lord your God and you will be able to stand firm... and you will succeed.*
> — 2 Chron. 20:20 (NLT)

You Are So Much Closer than You Think

The book *Three Feet from Gold* by Sharon Lechter and Greg Reid is an inspiring story about not falling down before the finish line. It tells of gold miners who dug and dug for a very long time with no success in finding the gold that they once had. They gave up and abandoned the site, sold their machinery, and simply walked away. Sure enough, another digger came to the same site with his own tools and started to dig three feet from the very spot that had previously been abandoned. Gold and fortune were found! I think the story speaks for itself.

> *Let us throw off everything that hinders and the sin that so easily entangles, and let us run with perseverance the race marked out for us.*
> — Heb. 12:1 (NIV)

You may be so close to reaching your goals that you'll get there soon if you just persevere. You get tired, yes. But God will renew your strength to keep going if you ask Him. If you are exhausted, worn out, and frustrated, then just hold on. Wait for the next wave of strength and then keep moving! You may be eighty-five years old when you feel you have completed your goals. So be it. Achieving a goal is achieving a goal! Isn't that what life is all about? Life is a journey. The true finish line is not crossed until you leave this earth, and then you will have a new life to live. While you are on this earth, you must finish your race.

Use all of the principles in this book—Sound Thought, Always Believe, and Life of Excellence—to get to where you need to be. You will get there. And then you will find peace.

> *Jesus knew that His mission was now finished, and to fulfill the Scripture He said, "I am thirsty." A jar of sour wine was sitting there, so they soaked a sponge in it, put it on a hyssop branch, and held it up to His lips. When Jesus had tasted it, he said, "It is finished!" Then he bowed His head and released His spirit.* — John 19:28–30 (NLT)

Prayer to Fulfill Your Dreams and Visions

Dear God,

Help me to fully understand what you have put in my heart from birth. Thank you for creating me for a special purpose and allowing me to be a part of your grand plan. When I falter, pick me up, renew my strength, and help me to once again figure out what you would have me do. Please give me patience. Thank you for providing what I need to fulfill the work you would have me do. Along the way, if I need to be taught some things, I will humbly accept the lessons you have in store for me as I know that in the end, I will be a better person for it and will be more equipped to do your will. Give me the endurance to finish my tasks in this lifetime, no matter how long it takes. I surrender to your way and your timing, not mine. When I am lonely and confused and feel as though the world is coming against me, I will focus on you and you alone. It is you that is always with me, even when I feel as if no one else believes in me. I will finish my race for you, God. Amen.

The World Shares the Goals of Love and Forgiveness

Jesus Christ and Christianity: "Love one another." "For if you forgive other people when they sin against you, your heavenly Father will also forgive you." "God is love." "Share your food with the hungry and ... provide the poor wanderer with shelter."

Near-Death Experience: Reports indicate that all that matters is how we treat others. We are all here for a purpose. Love is the essence of life. Compassion, forgiveness, and an overwhelming sense of love and joy radiate from a loving being.

Modern Psychology: Dr. Martin Seligman's goals are to move psychology from the ego to philanthropy. Altruism (giving) and kindness are crucial to happiness.

Science: Forgiveness and love improve cell function, boost the immune system, lower blood pressure, and reduce and/or eliminate the toxic chemicals that are released from the brain into the body, ultimately fighting disease and improving overall health.

Islam: Encourage the wealthy to give to the poor and needy. The purpose of existence is to love and serve God. Efface sin, forgive, and let sinners go unpunished. Everyone helps others.

Bahá'í: True love for others means seeing the beauty of God in other people; loving all humans regardless of race, religion, or community; and loving one's enemies.

Buddhism: Show compassion and mercy and reduce the suffering of others. Have an unconditional, unselfish interest in others' welfare.

Judaism: Have grace, goodwill, kindness, and compassion for fellow man and animals. Giving to the poor and needy, whether the need is physical or financial, is important.

Hinduism: Give selflessly, not expecting anything in return. Exclude no one; accept those from all walks of life. Emphasize love and peace.

Scientology: While scientology is not God-centered, it teaches godly principles such as loving and helping children and one's parents, treating others the way they would want to be treated, helping the environment, and respecting all religious beliefs.

Unification Church: There exists only one eternal God of infinite intelligence, whose nature is love and goodness. We should be united together with our minds in perfect harmony with God's love. Interfaith activities remove barriers between religions. Man's relationship with God is to be restored. Understanding of science and the nature of God are to become one. The kingdom of God on earth will be established as it is in heaven.

Chapter Six

My Expectations for STABLE: One World

The God of the whole earth shall he be called.
— Is. 54:5 (KJV)

As the book comes to a close, I must share with you my dream and vision for STABLE. It is my deepest desire that it is a blessing to you, and I hope that you apply these principles to your life. It is my only aspiration that you use them to aid you in reaching your highest and fullest potential and seeing through to completion what God has planned for you. To summarize, yes, I want to see souls healed and thriving. But the ultimate goal for STABLE is to bring forth an even stronger awareness of the spiritual world; that all of the consistencies of the death and revival experience become a vehicle to not only restore joy but to unite all nations of the world in peace as our barriers are no more.

From studies of near-death experiences, we have learned that heaven is a place where there is only joy; laughter; and positive, loving, and understanding compassion. It is a place where there is no sadness, doubt, depression, judgment, violence, fear, or cruelty. I imagine a day when we realize that our human bodies thrive and flourish physically when we think and behave in heavenly ways, not carnal and earthly ways. I imagine a day when we can laugh at the thoughts that contradict heavenly characteristics and see right through the veil into the true realities of heaven, making it quite easy to live out the STABLE philosophy. I imagine a day when the way we operate in this world will be completely reversed and viewed from the eternal perspective, not with the intention to obsess over death but to live better lives.

Jesus Christ's message is everywhere. It is in pop culture and modern psychology. His message of love and forgiveness has been backed up by scientific study of the health benefits that they bring to the human body, the "peace" He said we could have. His messages of love and giving can also be found as the core values of many of the world's organized religions and in ancient philosophies. I love Jesus, and He has saved me because He has given me an example of perseverance, courage, and endurance even when I am in incredible pain. He is not an icon, as He is too often viewed, but one who walked this earth and was ahead of His time. He knew what He was talking about, and He was an authority on how to thrive here on earth. That is why He is a Savior.

Motivational speakers, psychologists, and leaders of other religions present similar messages. The world has a shared message. Let us come to realize that we all have common goals, values, and beliefs; break down the walls of religion; and finally admit that we all want the same thing and essentially believe in the same thing. If you do not consider Jesus to be a personal Savior, then believe in his works and teachings because they hold true today more than ever. His teachings truly do overcome the world. They lift the deception from the world, which is on a path that is clearly leading to depression and disease, as the World Health Organization reports.

This is not an us-versus-them message. This is a call for the entire world to come together. I, as a Christian, embrace the loving and godly values of Islam, Buddhism, Scientology, and the like because that is what Jesus did. The Jesus I know was all things to all people. The Jesus I know turned no one away. That is love in its truest form. I am asking people of the world to do the same.

> *If we have not achieved peace, it is because people forget its most fundamental aspect.*
> — Rev. Sun Myung Moon

We are a world that is living in complete contrast to the basic cores of our religions. We are a consuming world, piling up material belongings that will be gone in an instant. That is not reality. It is an illusion. We live with a discriminating mentality, and we cling to our own kind.

We mock, judge, hate, and even kill those who are not like us and who do not share our traditions or dress like we do. We do not accept ourselves. We label ourselves as belonging to one affiliation or another. We complain. We bully. We sue. It is devastating how much suffering and sadness there is in the world. And yet, we just want more, more, more. We give up when things are not going perfectly. Isaiah 45:18 says, "God made the world to be lived in, not an empty place of chaos." And what an empty place of chaos it has become.

What baffles me is that as a human race, we have become so highly advanced. We get information and communication in the blink of an eye. We have the Internet, smartphones, cures for diseases, modern conveniences, and the ability to travel into outer space. And yet, when it comes to religions against religions—well, this is the one area in which we remain frozen in barbarity. In the worlds of business, technology, medicine, and travel, we have no difficulties collaborating at the conference table. The sharing of new discoveries and ideas in these areas is commonplace. We keep improving and innovating, and now is an amazing time to be alive. Computers, televisions, automobiles, medicines, diagnostics, home conveniences, and so on get better and better with the sharing of ideas. Why, then, can we not collaborate in the area of religion? Why is the world so segregated? Why can't we do the same thing that we do with other modern innovations and work together regarding our spirituality? How do we finally break down the barriers? It is time to try a new approach. It is time to undo what we are doing.

This is our cry. This is our prayer. Peace in the world. —The plaque on the statue of Sadako Sasaki that stands in the Hiroshima Peace Memorial Park. Sadako died at age twelve from the effects of the atomic bomb that was dropped on August 6, 1945. She is now a primary symbol of the impact of nuclear war. Thousands of people pray for world peace at her statue every year.

We hold in our hands a key to peace on earth, yet it has been overlooked. It is the near-death experience. It must be examined closely by every living human being. The near-death experience offers one common experience, and only one. It is time for the world to embrace this reality and come together in love.

> *The evidence suggesting that there is no significant difference in near-death experiences worldwide makes possible a major step forward in human relations.... We may be separated by languages and cultures, but the possibility of having similar spiritual experiences as dramatic and transformative as NDEs unites us around the world.... That makes NDEs an important spiritual concept that can help humanity strive toward world peace. The evidence that near-death experiences are basically the same* worldwide *may be a reason to stop bickering over differences and instead focus on our similarities.*
> — Dr. Jeffrey Long, *Evidence of the Afterlife*

There is one particular organized religion, which I will not name here, that embraces many of the principles mentioned in this book and does much good for society. However, it also makes this bold statement: "Despite its many successes, science has not provided answers to questions Man has been asking himself since time immemorial: Who are we? What do we consist of? Where do we come from? Where are we going? What are we doing?"

These are notions that I simply must disagree with. Science *is* answering all of these questions. I imagine a world that looks to science to back up the eternal truth of how we were meant to live in health and happiness. Colossians 3:1 (NLT) says, "Set your sights on the realities of heaven." The "realities" are loving, forgiving, giving of ourselves, helping others, thinking healthy thoughts, and so on. I implore you to research modern medical journals that report on such behavior. We utilize science to prove everything in this world before we accept it as truth. Look all around you at the directives from pop culture and secular teachers. We are bombarded with these same messages from all angles and yet we pick and choose who we name the authority. The realities of heaven are the ultimate truth. Heaven is speaking to us. Why won't we listen?

I am asking world leaders, political leaders, figureheads, spiritual teachers, religious leaders, scientists, near-death experience researchers, and psychologists to come together and examine the true qualities of heaven. I am asking our leaders and every one of you to create a oneness, a global understanding of where we all come from, where we are all going, and why we are here. Let us live as though heaven is on earth and finally answer the Pope's question of "How can science contribute to peace on earth?"

I imagine a world where we live in ways that were engineered by our Creator and where we use these principles to stop destroying ourselves, our planet, and all of its living creatures. I see a world where we all acknowledge that there is one God for the entire world, as the near-death experience offers only one version, and a day on which we can all communicate with Him openly and use our instincts to hear Him. I imagine a world in which people recognize their gifts and talents and work with God over and over again until they find their true purpose and carry it out to completion. I envision a time when the middle class and wealthy people see the overwhelming surplus that they really have, find the beauty and blessings in simple things, and realize just how few material things they really need; it is a time when they share all that they have with their hurting and even starving neighbors. I imagine a world of no judgment or hate, a world where we all acknowledge everyone's story and understand why people suffer and lash out, a world where we no longer internalize hurt and seek revenge but understand and forgive. I imagine a world that understands that the afterlife holds no labels or spiritual segregation and in which the walls of conflict come crumbling down; a world in which the murdering of each other over our differences ceases to exist. I hope for a world where the global burden of disease caused by depression is attacked at its very core and becomes a reality of the past.

I imagine a world where politicians, scientists, psychologists, and religious and world leaders bring their knowledge to a table of collaboration, validating all of the mutual cores of their religions, and peace is finally obtained. It is not impossible. It's not. I believe. We are a highly intelligent people, a highly intelligent human race worldwide. Anything other than that makes no sense whatsoever. This is just smart. It is time to evolve.

> *It has come at last—salvation and power and the Kingdom of our God.* — Rev. 12:10 (NLT)

Final Thoughts from the Author

I want to also communicate to you that anything can be addictive. Listening to speakers like myself and reading inspiring books can temporarily make us feel warm and fuzzy. I ask that you train yourself in the STABLE philosophy for as long as you feel you need to. Eventually, however, you need to put the books down, stop listening, and go live it out. Put these principles into action. Otherwise, they are nothing but words on a page. God bless you. And thank you.

Printed in the United States
By Bookmasters